Travellers' French

D. L. Ellis, F. Clark

Pronunciation **Dr J. Baldwin**

Je parle
tu parles
il parle

Pan Books London and Sydney

The publishers would like to thank the French Tourist
Office for their help during the preparation of this book

First published 1981 by Pan Books Ltd,
Cavaye Place, London SW10 9PG

4 5 6 7 8 9

© D. L. Ellis and F. Clark 1981
ISBN 0 330 26292 0
Printed and bound in Great Britain by
Hunt Barnard Printing Ltd., Aylesbury, Bucks.

Contents

Using the phrase book

- This phrase book is designed to help you get by in France, to get what you want or need. It concentrates on the simplest but most effective way you can express these needs in an unfamiliar language.
- The CONTENTS on p. 5 give you a good idea of which section to consult for the phrase you need.
- The INDEX on p. 151 gives more detailed information about where to look for your phrase.
- When you have found the right page you will be given:
  either – the exact phrase
      or – help in making up a suitable sentence
     and – help in getting the pronunciation right
- The English sentences in **bold type** will be useful for you in a variety of different situations, so they are worth learning by heart. (See also DO IT YOURSELF p. 142.)
- Wherever possible you will find help in understanding what French people say to *you*, in reply to your questions.
- If you want to practise the basic nuts and bolts of the language further, look at the DO IT YOURSELF section starting on p. 142.
- Note especially these three sections:
    Everyday expressions p. 11
    Shop talk p. 54
    Public notices p. 121
  You are sure to want to refer to them most frequently.
- When you arrive in France make good use of the tourist information offices (see p. 23).

  UK address: French Tourist Office
                178 Piccadilly, London W1

A note on the pronunciation system

It is usual in phrase books for there to be a pronunciation section, which tries to teach English-speaking tourists how to pronounce correctly the language of the country they are visiting. Such attempts are based on the argument that correct pronunciation is essential for comprehension. The system in this book, however, is founded on three quite different assumptions: firstly, that it is not possible to describe in print the sounds of a foreign language in such a way that the English speaker with no phonetic training will produce them accurately, or even intelligibly; secondly, that perfect pronunciation is not essential for communication, and lastly that the average visitor abroad is more interested in achieving successful communication than in learning how to pronounce new speech sounds. Observation and experience have shown these assumptions to be justified. The most important characteristic of the present system, therefore, is that it makes no attempt whatsoever to teach the sounds of the other language, but uses instead the nearest English sounds to them. The sentences transcribed for pronunciation are designed to be read as naturally as possible, as if they were ordinary English (of a generally southeastern English variety), and with no attempt to make the words sound 'foreign'. In this way you will still sound quite English, but you will at the same time be understood. Practice always helps performance, and it is a good idea to rehearse aloud any of the sentences you know you are going to need. When you do come to the point of using them, say them with conviction.

In French it is important to read each syllable with equal emphasis. For instance, in the following English example we have ten syllables and ten stresses: Little Jack Horner sat in the corner. Though this will probably sound rather mechanical to an English ear, it will help the French speaker to understand you.

Of course you may enjoy trying to pronounce a foreign language as well as possible and the present system is a good way to start. However, since it only uses the sounds of English, you will very soon need to depart from it as you begin to imitate the sounds you hear the native speaker produce and to relate them to the spelling of the other language. Be prepared, however, for the relationship between pronunciation and spelling to be a complex one.

Bon courage!

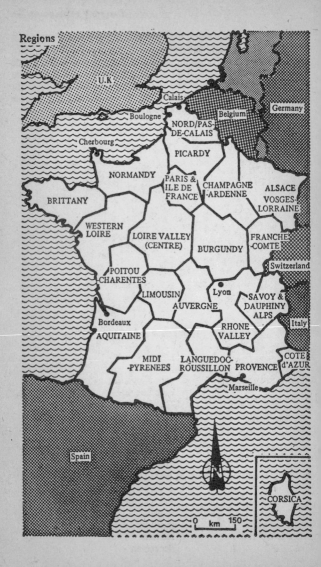

Regions

U.K

Calais

Boulogne

Cherbourg

NORD/PAS-
DE-CALAIS

Belgium

Germany

PICARDY

NORMANDY

BRITTANY

PARIS &
ILE DE
FRANCE

CHAMPAGNE
-ARDENNE

ALSACE
VOSGES-
LORRAINE

WESTERN
LOIRE

LOIRE VALLEY
(CENTRE)

BURGUNDY

FRANCHE-
COMTE

Switzerland

POITOU
CHARENTES

LIMOUSIN

Lyon

AUVERGNE

SAVOY &
DAUPHINY
ALPS

Italy

Bordeaux

AQUITAINE

RHONE
VALLEY

MIDI
-PYRENEES

LANGUEDOC-
ROUSSILLON

PROVENCE

COTE
d'AZUR

Marseille

Spain

N

0   km   150

CORSICA

Everyday expressions

[See also 'Shop talk' p. 54]

Hello	**Bonjour**
Good morning	bonshoor
Good day	**Salut** (friends only)
Good afternoon	saloo
Good evening	**Bonsoir**
	bonswah
Good night	**Bonne nuit**
	bon nwee
Goodbye	**Au revoir**
	o-revwah
See you later	**A tout à l'heure**
	ah tootahler
Yes	**Oui**
	wee
Please	**S'il vous plaît**
	sil voo pleh
Yes, please	**Oui, s'il vous plaît**
	wee sil voo pleh
Great!	**Formidable!**
	for-mee-dab
Thank you	**Merci**
	mair-see
Thank you very much	**Merci beaucoup**
	mair-see bo-coo
That's right	**C'est exact**
	set exah
No	**Non**
	non
No, thank you	**Non, merci**
	non mair-see

('Merci' by itself can also mean 'No thank you.')

I disagree	**Je ne suis pas d'accord**
	sher ner swee pah dah-cor
Excuse me	**Pardon**
Sorry	par-don
Don't mention it	**De rien**
That's OK	der ree-an

That's good ⎤	**Ça va**
I like it ⎦	sah vah
That's no good ⎤	**Ça ne va pas**
I don't like it ⎦	sah ner vah pah
I know	**Je sais**
	sher seh
I don't know	**Je ne sais pas**
	sher ner seh pah
It doesn't matter	**Ça ne fait rien**
	sah ner feh ree-an
Where's the toilet, please?	**Où sont les WC, s'il vous plaît?**
	oo son leh veh-seh sil voo pleh
How much is that? [*point*]	**C'est combien, ça?**
	seh combee-an sah
Is the service included?	**Est-ce que le service est compris?**
	esk ler sairvees eh compree
Do you speak English?	**Parlez-vous anglais?**
	parleh-voo ahngleh
I'm sorry ...	**Je regrette ...**
	sher rer-gret ...
I don't speak French	**je ne parle pas français**
	sher ner parl pah frahn-seh
I only speak a little French	**je parle très peu le français**
	sher parl treh per ler frahn-seh
I don't understand	**je ne comprends pas**
	sher ner comprahn pah
Please can you ...	**S'il vous plaît, pouvez-vous ...**
	sil voo pleh pooveh-voo ...
repeat that?	**répéter?**
	reh-peh-teh
speak more slowly?	**parler plus lentement?**
	parleh ploo lahnt-mahn
write it down?	**l'écrire?**
	leh-creer
What is this called in French? [*point*]	**Comment ça s'appelle en français?**
	commahn sah sappel ahn frahn-seh

Crossing the border

ESSENTIAL INFORMATION

- Don't waste time just before you leave rehearsing what you're going to say to the border officials – the chances are that you won't have to say anything at all, especially if you travel by air.
- It's more useful to check that you have your documents handy for the journey: passport, tickets, money, travellers' cheques, insurance documents, driving licence and car registration documents.
- Look out for these signs:
  DOUANE (customs)
  FRONTIÈRE (border)
  [*For further signs and notices, see p. 121*.]
- You may be asked routine questions by the customs officials [*see below*]. If you have to give personal details see 'Meeting people', p. 14. The other important answer to know is
  'Nothing': **Rien** (ree-an).

ROUTINE QUESTIONS

Passport?	**Passeport?**
	passpor
Insurance?	**Assurance?**
	assoo-rahns
Registration document?	**Carte grise?**
(logbook)	cart greez
Ticket, please	**Billet, s'il vous plaît**
	bee-yeh sil voo pleh
Have you anything to declare?	**Avez-vous quelque chose à déclarer?**
	ahveh-voo kelk shoz ah deh-clah-reh
Where are you going?	**Où allez-vous?**
	oo alleh-voo
How long are you staying?	**Combien de temps comptez-vous rester?**
	combee-an der tahn conteh-voo resteh
Where have you come from?	**D'où venez-vous?**
	doo ver-neh voo

You may also have to fill in forms which ask for:

surname	nom
first name	prénom
maiden name	nom de jeune fille
date of birth	date de naissance
place of birth	lieu de naissance
address	adresse
nationality	nationalité
profession	profession
passport number	numéro du passeport
issued at	fait à
signature	signature

Meeting People

[See also 'Everyday expressions', p. 11.]

Breaking the ice

Hello ⎤
Good morning ⎦

Bonjour (Salut)
bonshoor (saloo)

(The above bracketed expression should only be used with people you know well.)

How are you?

Ça va?
sah vah

Pleased to meet you

Enchanté/e
ahn-shahn-teh

I am here . . .

Je suis ici . . .
sher swee ee-see . . .

on holiday

en vacances
ahn vahcahns

on business

pour affaires
poor affair

Can I offer you . . .

Puis-je vous offrir . . .
pweesh vooz offreer . . .

a drink?

un verre?
an vair

a cigarette?

une cigarette?
oon cigarette

a cigar?	**un cigare?**
	an cigar
Are you staying long?	**Vous êtes ici pour longtemps*?**
	voozet ee-see poor longtahn

Name

What is your name?	**Comment vous appelez-vous?**
	commahn vooz appleh-voo
My name is ...	**Je m'appelle ...**
	shmappel ...

Family

Are you married?	**Vous êtes marié/e*?**
	voozet maree-eh
I am ...	**Je suis ...**
	sher swee ...
married	**marié/e***
	maree-eh
single	**célibataire**
	cehlee-batair
This is ...	**Voici ...**
	vwah-see ...
my wife	**ma femme**
	mah fam
my husband	**mon mari**
	mon maree
my daughter	**ma fille**
	mah fee
my son	**mon fils**
	mon feess
my (boy) friend	**mon ami**
	mon-ahmee
my (girl) friend	**mon amie**
	mon-ahmee
my (male) colleague	**mon collègue**
	mon colleg
my (female) colleague	**ma collègue**
	mah colleg

* Use the first alternative for men, the second for women.

Do you have any children?	**Avez-vous des enfants?**
	ahveh-voo dez-ahnfahn
I have ...	**J'ai ...**
	sheh ...
one daughter	**une fille**
	oon fee
one son	**un fils**
	an feess
two daughters	**deux filles**
	der fee
three sons	**trois fils**
	trwah feess
No, I haven't any children	**Non je n'ai pas d'enfants**
	non sher neh pah dahnfahn

Where you live

Are you ...	**Vous êtes ...**
	voozet ...
Belgian?	**belge?**
	belsh
French?	**français/e?***
	frahn-seh/-sez
from Luxembourg?	**du Luxembourg?**
	doo look-sahn-boor
Swiss?	**suisse?**
	sweess
I am ...	**Je suis ...**
	sher swee ...
American	**américain/e***
	american/-ken
English	**anglais/e***
	angleh/-glez

[*For other nationalities, see p. 134.*]

I live ...	**J'habite ...**
	shahbeet ...
in London	**Londres**
	lond
in England	**l'Angleterre**
	lahng-tair

* Use the first alternative for men, the second for women.

in the north	**dans le nord** dahn ler nor
in the south	**dans le sud** dahn ler sood
in the east	**dans l'est** dahn lest
in the west	**dans l'ouest** dahn looest
in the centre	**dans le centre** dahn ler sahnt

[*For other countries, see p. 134.*]

For the businessman and woman

I'm from . . . (firm's name)	**Je travaille pour . . .** sher trah-vy poor . . .
I have an appointment with . . .	**J'ai rendez-vous avec . . .** sheh rahndeh-voo ahvec . . .
May I speak to . . . ?	**Puis-je parler à . . . ?** pweesh parleh ah . . .
This is my card	**Voici ma carte** vwah-see mah cart
I'm sorry I'm late	**Je m'excuse d'être en retard** sher mexcooz det ahn rer-tar
Can I fix another appointment?	**Puis-je prendre un autre rendez-vous?** pweesh prahnd an ot rahndeh-voo
I'm staying at the (Paris) hotel	**Je suis à l'hôtel (Paris)** sher swee a lotel (pahree)
I'm staying in (St John's) road	**Je suis dans la rue (St Jean)** sher swee dahn lah roo (san-shahn)

Asking the way

ESSENTIAL INFORMATION

- Keep a look out for all these place names as you will find them on shops, maps and notices.

WHAT TO SAY

Excuse me, please	**Pardonnez-moi, s'il vous plaît** par-do-neh mwah sil voo pleh
How do I get ...	**Pour aller ...** poor alleh ...
to Paris?	**à Paris?** ah pahree
to rue St Pierre?	**à la rue Saint-Pierre?** ah lah roo san-pee-air
to the hotel Metropole?	**à l'hôtel Métropole?** ah lotel meh-tro-pol
to the airport?	**à l'aéroport?** ah lah-eh-ropor
to the beach?	**à la plage?** ah lah plash
to the bus station?	**à la gare d'autobus?** ah lah gar dotoboos
to the historic site?	**au site historique?** o seet eestoreek
to the market?	**au maché?** o marsheh
to the police station?	**au commissariat?** o commissaree-ah
to the port?	**au port?** o por
to the post office?	**à la poste?** ah lah post
to the railway station?	**à la gare?** ah lah gar
to the sports stadium?	**au stade?** o stad

to the tourist information office?	**au syndicat d'initiative?**
	o sandeecah dinisee-ativ
to the town centre?	**au centre de la ville?**
	o sahnt der lah veel
to the town hall?	**à la mairie?**
	ah lah mai-ree
Excuse me, please	**Pardonnez-moi, s'il vous plaît**
	par-do-neh mwah sil voo pleh
Is there . . . near by?	**Est-ce qu'il y a . . . près d'ici?**
	eskil yah . . . preh dee-see
an art gallery	**un musée d'art**
	an moozeh dar
a baker's	**une boulangerie**
	oon boolahn-shree
a bank	**une banque**
	oon bahnk
a bar	**un bar**
	an bar
a botanical garden	**un jardin botanique**
	an shardan botah-neek
a bus stop	**un arrêt d'autobus**
	an ahreh dotoboos
a butcher's	**une boucherie**
	oon booshree
a café	**un café**
	an cahfeh
a cake shop	**une pâtisserie**
	oon pahteess-ree
a campsite	**un camping**
	an camping
a car park	**un parking**
	an parking
a change bureau	**un bureau de change**
	an buro der shahnsh
a chemist's	**une pharmacie**
	oon pharmacy
a church	**une église**
	oon eh-gleez
a cinema	**un cinéma**
	an cinema
a delicatessen	**une charcuterie**
	oon sharcootree

Is there . . . near by?   **Est-ce qu'il y a . . . près d'ici?**
eskil yah . . . preh dee-see

a dentist's   **un dentiste**
an dahnteest

a department store   **un grand magasin**
an grahn mahgahzan

a disco   **une discothèque**
oon discotek

a doctor's surgery   **un docteur**
an doc-ter

a dry cleaner's   **un pressing**
an pressing

a fishmonger's   **une poissonnerie**
oon pwah-son-ree

a garage (for repairs)   **un garage**
an gahrash

a hairdresser's   **un coiffeur**
an kwah-fer

a greengrocer's   **un marchand de légumes**
an marshahn der lehgoom

a grocer's   **une épicerie**
oon ehpeess-ree

a hardware shop   **une quincaillerie**
oon kan-kay-ree

a Health and Social Security Office   **un bureau de la Sécurité Sociale**
an buro der lah sehcooreeteh sossee-al

a hospital   **un hôpital**
an opeetal

a hotel   **un hôtel**
an otel

a hypermarket   **un hypermarché**
an eepair-marsheh

a laundry   **une laverie**
oon lav-ree

a museum   **un musée**
an moo-zeh

a newsagent's   **un marchand de journaux**
an marshahn der shoorno

a night club   **une boîte de nuit**
oon bwaht der nwee

a petrol station   **une station service**
oon stah-see-on sairvees

a post box	**une boîte à lettres**
	oon bwaht ah let
a public garden (town park)	**un jardin public**
	an shardan poobleek
a public telephone	**un téléphone**
	an telefon
a public toilet	**des WC publics**
	deh veh-seh poobleek
a restaurant	**un restaurant**
	an restorahn
a snack bar	**un snack**
	an snack
a sports ground	**un terrain de sport**
	an terran der spor
a supermarket	**un supermarché**
	an soopair-marsheh
a sweet shop	**une confiserie**
	oon confeez-ree
a swimming pool	**une piscine**
	oon pee-seen
a taxi stand	**une station de taxis**
	oon stah-see-on der taxee
a theatre	**un théâtre**
	an teh-aht
a tobacconist's	**un bureau de tabac**
	an buro der tahbah
a travel agent's	**une agence de voyage**
	oon ashahns der vwah-yash
a youth hostel	**une auberge de jeunesse**
	oon obairsh der sher-ness
a zoo	**un zoo**
	an zo-o

DIRECTIONS

- Asking where a place is, or if a place is nearby, is one thing; making sense of the answer is another.
- Here are some of the most important key directions and replies.

Left	**Gauche**
	goshe
Right	**Droite**
	drwaht

22/Asking the way

Straight on	**Tout droit**
	too drwah
There	**Là**
	lah
First left/right	**La première rue à gauche/droite**
	lah prem-yair roo ah goshe/drwaht
Second left/right	**La deuxième rue à gauche/droite**
	lah der-zee-em roo ah goshe/drwaht
At the crossroads	**Au carrefour**
	o carfoor
At the traffic lights	**Aux feux**
	o fer
At the roundabout	**Au rond-point**
	o ron-pwen
At the level-crossing	**Au passage à niveau**
	o passash ah neevo
It's near/far	**C'est près/loin**
	seh preh/lwen
One kilometre	**Un kilomètre**
	an keelomet
Two kilometres	**Deux kilomètres**
	der keelomet
Five minutes . . .	**Cinq minutes . . .**
	sank meenoot . . .
on foot	**à pied**
	ah pee-eh
by car	**en voiture**
	ahn vwah-toor
Take . . .	**Prenez . . .**
	prer-neh . . .
the bus	**l'autobus**
	lotoboos
the train	**le train**
	ler tran
the tram	**le tram**
	ler tram
the underground	**le métro**
	ler metro

[*For public transport, see p. 112.*]

The tourist information office

ESSENTIAL INFORMATION

- Most towns and even some villages in France have a tourist information office, run by the regional or local tourist boards.
- Look for these words:
  SYNDICAT D'INITIATIVE
  OFFICE DE TOURISME
- Sometimes there may be signposts with these abbreviations: **SI**, **OT** or **ESSI**.
- Information is also available from the Touring Club and Automobile Club offices, often indicated with the abbreviations **TCF** (French Touring Club) and **ACF** (French Automobile Club). **TCF** also offers a breakdown service **Touring Secours.**
- These offices give you free information in the form of printed leaflets, fold-outs, brochures, lists and plans.
- You may have to pay for some of these but this is not usual.
- For finding a tourist office, see p. 18.

WHAT TO SAY

Please, have you got . . .

S'il vous plaît, avez-vous . . .
sil voo pleh ahveh-voo . . .

a plan of the town?

un plan de la ville?
an plahn der lah veel

a list of hotels?

une liste d'hôtels?
oon leest dotel

a list of campsites?

une liste de campings?
oon leest der camping

a list of restaurants?

une liste de restaurants?
oon leest der restorahn

a list of coach excursions?

une liste d'excursions en car?
oon leest dexcoor-see-on an car

a list of events?

une liste d'événements?
oon leest deh-veh-ner-mahn

a leaflet on the town?

une brochure sur la ville?
oon broshooer soor lah veel

Please, have you got . . .	**S'il vous plaît, avez-vous . . .** sil voo pleh ahveh-voo . . .
a leaflet on the region?	**une brochure sur la région?** oon broshooer soor lah resh-yon
a railway timetable?	**un horaire des trains?** an orair deh tran
a bus timetable?	**un horaire des autobus?** an orair deh zotoboos
In English, please	**En anglais, s'il vous plaît** ahn ahngleh sil voo pleh
How much do I owe you?	**Combien vous dois-je?** combee-an voo dwahsh
Can you recommend . . .	**Pouvez-vous recommander . . .** pooveh-voo rer-commahndeh . . .
a cheap hotel?	**un hôtel bon marché?** an otel bon marsheh
a cheap restaurant?	**un restaurant bon marché?** an restorahn bon marsheh
Can you make a booking for me?	**Pouvez-vous me faire une réservation?** pooveh-voo mer fair oon rehzairvah-see-on

LIKELY ANSWERS

You need to understand when the answer is 'No'. You should be able to tell by the assistant's facial expression, tone of voice and gesture, but there are some language clues, such as:

No	**Non** non
I'm sorry	**Je regrette** sher rer-gret
I don't have a list of campsites	**Je n'ai pas la liste des campings** sher neh pah lah leest deh camping
I haven't got any left	**Il ne m'en reste plus** il ner mahn rest ploo
It's free	**C'est gratuit** seh grah-twee

Accommodation

Hotel

ESSENTIAL INFORMATION

- If you want hotel-type accommodation, all the following words
  in capital letters are worth looking for on name boards:
  HÔTEL
  MOTEL
  PENSION (a small, privately run hotel)
  AUBERGE (often picturesque type of hotel situated in the
  countryside)
- Lists of hotels and **pensions** can be obtained from local tourist
  offices or the French Tourist Office in London [*see p. 23*].
- The cost is displayed in the room itself, so you can check it when
  having a look round before agreeing to stay.
- The displayed cost is for the room itself, per night and not per
  person. Breakfast is extra, and therefore optional.
- Not all hotels provide meals, apart from breakfast. A **pension**
  always provides meals. Breakfast is continental style: coffee or
  tea with rolls/croissants, butter and jam.
- An identity document is requested when registering at a hotel and
  will normally be kept overnight. Passports or driving licences are
  accepted.
- Tipping: Look for the words **service compris/non compris** (service
  included/not included) on your bill. Tip porters.
- Finding a hotel, see p. 18.

WHAT TO SAY

I have a booking	**J'ai une réservation** sheh oon rehzairvah-see-on

Have you any vacancies,
  please?
	Avez-vous des chambres libres,
	  s'il vous plaît?
	ahveh-voo deh shahmb leeb sil
	  voo pleh

Can I book a room?	**Puis-je réserver une chambre?**
	pweesh rehzairveh oon shahmb
It's for ...	**C'est pour ...**
	seh poor ...
one person	**une personne**
	oon pairson
two people	**deux personnes**
	der pairson

[*For numbers, see p. 126.*]

It's for ...	**C'est pour ...**
	seh poor ...
one night	**une nuit**
	oon nwee
two nights	**deux nuits**
	der nwee
one week	**une semaine**
	oon ser-men
two weeks	**deux semaines**
	der ser-men
I would like ...	**Je voudrais ...**
	sher voodreh ...
a (quiet) room	**une chambre (tranquille)**
	oon shahmb (trahnkeel)
two rooms	**deux chambres**
	der shahmb
with a single bed	**à un lit**
	ah an lee
with two single beds	**à deux lits**
	ah der lee
with a double bed	**avec un grand lit**
	ahvec an grahn lee
with a toilet	**avec WC**
	ahvec veh-seh
with a bathroom	**avec salle de bains**
	ahvec sal der ban
with a shower	**avec douche**
	ahvec doosh
with a cot	**avec un lit d'enfant**
	ahvec an lee dahnfahn
with a balcony	**avec balcon**
	ahvec bal-con

I would like ...

    full board

    half board

    bed and breakfast

[See essential information]

Do you serve meals?

At what time is ...

    breakfast?

    lunch?

    dinner?

How much is it?

Can I look at the room?

I'd prefer a room ...

    at the front/at the back

OK, I'll take it

No thanks, I won't take it

The key to number (10), please

Please, can I have ...

    a coat hanger?

    a towel?

    a glass?

Je voudrais ...
sher voodreh

pension complète
pahn-see-on complet

demi-pension
der-me pahn-see-on

chambre et petit déjeuner
shahmb eh ptee desh-neh

Est-ce que vous faites restaurant?
esk voo fet restorahn

A quelle heure est ...
ah keller eh ...

le petit déjeuner?
ler ptee desh-neh

le déjeuner?
ler desh-neh

le dîner?
ler dee-neh

C'est combien?
seh combee-an

Puis-je voir la chambre?
pweesh vwah lah shahmb

J'aimerais mieux une chambre ...
shem-reh me-er oon shahmb ...

sur le devant/derrière
soor ler der-vahn/derri-air

D'accord, je la prends
daccor sher lah prahn

Non merci, je ne la prends pas
non mair-see sher ner lah prahn pah

La clé du (dix), s'il vous plaît
lah cleh doo (deess) sil voo pleh

S'il vous plaît, puis-je avoir ...
sil voo pleh pweesh ahvwah ...

un cintre?
an sant

une serviette?
oon sairv-yet

un verre?
an vair

Please, can I have ...	S'il vous plaît, puis-je avoir ...
	Sil voo pleh pweesh ahvwah ...
some soap?	du savon?
	doo sav-on
an ashtray?	un cendrier?
	an sahndree-eh
another pillow?	un autre oreiller?
	an ot oreh-yeh
another blanket?	une autre couverture?
	oon ot coovairtoor
Come in!	Entrez!
	ahntreh
One moment, please!	Un moment, s'il vous plaît!
	an mo-mahn sil voo pleh
Please can you ...	S'il vous plaît, pouvez-vous ...
	sil voo pleh pooveh voo ...
do this laundry/dry-cleaning?	laver ceci/nettoyer ceci?
	lav-eh ser-see/nettwah-yeh ser-see
call me at ... ?	m'appeler à ... ?
	mappleh ah ...
help me with my luggage?	m'aider à porter mes bagages?
	med-eh ah porteh meh baggash
call me a taxi for ... ?	m'appeler un taxi pour ... ?
	mappleh an taxee poor ...

[*For times, see p. 128.*]

The bill, please	La note, s'il vous plaît
	lah not sil voo pleh
Is service included?	Est-ce que le service est compris?
	esk ler sairvees eh compree
I think this is wrong	Je crois qu'il y a une erreur
	sher crwah kil yah oon error
May I have a receipt?	Puis-je avoir un reçu?
	pweesh ahvwah oon rer-soo

At breakfast

Some more ... please	Encore ... s'il vous plaît
	ahncor ... sil voo pleh
coffee	du café
	doo cahfeh

tea	**du thé**
	doo teh
bread	**du pain**
	doo pan
butter	**du beurre**
	doo ber
jam	**de la confiture**
	der lah confeetoor
May I have a boiled egg?	**Puis-je avoir un œuf à la coque?**
	pweesh ahvwah an erf ah lah cok

LIKELY REACTIONS

Have you an identity document, please?	**Avez-vous une pièce d'identité, s'il vous plaît?**
	ahveh-voo oon pee-ess deedahn-teeteh sil voo pleh
What's your name? [see p. 11]	**Quel est votre nom?**
	kel eh vot nom
Sorry, we're full	**Je regrette, c'est complet**
	sher rer-gret seh compleh
I haven't any rooms left	**Je n'ai plus de chambres**
	sher neh ploo der shahmb
Do you want to have a look?	**Vous voulez voir?**
	voo vooleh vwah
How many people is it for?	**C'est pour combien de personnes?**
	seh poor combee-an der pairson
From (7 o'clock) onwards	**A partir de (sept) heures**
	ah parteer der (set) er
From (midday) onwards	**A partir de (midi)**
	ah parteer der (meedee)
[For times, see p. 128.]	
It's (63) francs	**C'est (soixante-trois) francs**
	seh (swah-sahnt trwah) frahn
[For numbers, see p. 126.]	

Camping and youth hostelling

ESSENTIAL INFORMATION
Camping

● Look for the word **CAMPING** or this sign.

● Be prepared to have to pay:
per person
for the car (if applicable)
for the tent or caravan plot
for electricity
for hot showers
● You must provide proof of identity such as your passport.
● You can obtain lists of campsites from local tourist offices [*see* p. 18] or from the French Tourist Office in London.
● Some campsites offer discounts to campers with the International Camping Carnet and some offer weekly, fortnightly or monthly rates.
● Officially recognized campsites have a star rating (like hotels).
● Municipal-run campsites are often reasonably priced and well-run.
● Off-site camping (**le camping sauvage**) is prohibited in many areas. As a rule it is better and safer to use recognized sites.

Youth hostels

● Look for the words: **AUBERGE DE JEUNESSE**.
● You will be asked for a YHA card and your passport on arrival.
● Food and cooking facilities vary from hostel to hostel and you may have to help with the domestic chores.
● You must take your own sleeping bag lining but sheets can usually be hired on arrival.
● In the high season it is advisable to book beds in advance, and

your stay will be limited to a maximum of three consecutive nights per hostel.
- Apply to the French Tourist Office in London or local tourist offices in France [see p. 18] for lists of youth hostels and details of regulations for hostellers.
- For buying or replacing camping equipment, see p. 52.

WHAT TO SAY

I have a booking	**J'ai une réservation**
	sheh oon rehzairvah-see-on
Have you any vacancies?	**Avez-vous de la place?**
	ahveh-voo der lah plass
It's for . . .	**C'est pour . . .**
	seh poor . . .
one adult/one person	**un adulte/une personne**
	an ahdoolt/oon pairson
two adults/two people	**deux adultes/deux personnes**
	der zahdoolt/der pairson
and one child	**et un enfant**
	eh an ahnfahn
and two children	**et deux enfants**
	eh der zahnfahn
It's for . . .	**C'est pour . . .**
	seh poor . . .
one night	**une nuit**
	oon nwee
two nights	**deux nuits**
	der nwee
one week	**une semaine**
	oon ser-men
two weeks	**deux semaines**
	der ser-men
How much is it . . .	**C'est combien . . .**
	seh combee-an . . .
for the tent?	**pour la tente?**
	poor lah tahnt
for the caravan?	**pour la caravane?**
	poor lah caravan
for the car?	**pour la voiture?**
	poor lah vwah-toor

How much is it . . .   **C'est combien . . .**
                            seh combee-an . . .

  for the electricity?   **pour l'électricité?**
                            poor leh-lectriciteh

  per person?   **par personne?**
                            par pairson

  per day/night? **par jour/nuit?**
                            par shoor/nwee

May I look round?   **Puis-je voir?**
                            pweesh vwah

Do you close the gate at   **Est-ce que vous fermez le portail**
  night?   **la nuit?**
                            esk-voo fairmeh ler por-ty lah
                            nwee

Do you provide anything . . .   **Est-ce qu'on peut avoir . . .**
                            eskon per ahvwah . . .

  to eat?   **de la nourriture?**
                            der lah nooreetoor

  to drink?   **des boissons?**
                            deh bwah-son

Is there/are there . . .   **Est-ce qu'il y a . . .**
                            eskil yah . . .

  a bar?   **un bar?**
                            an bar

  hot showers?   **des douches chaudes?**
                            deh doosh shod

  a kitchen?   **une cuisine?**
                            oon kweezeen

  a laundry?   **une laverie?**
                            oon lav-ree

  a restaurant?   **un restaurant?**
                            an restorahn

  a shop?   **un magasin?**
                            an mahgah-zan

  a swimming pool?   **une piscine?**
                            oon pee-seen

  a takeaway?   **des plats à emporter?**
                            deh plah ah ahmporteh

[*For food shopping, see p. 59, and for eating and drinking out, see p. 80.*]

I would like a counter for the shower	**Je voudrais un jeton pour la douche**
	sher voodreh an sher-ton poor lah doosh
Where are . . .	**Où sont . . .**
	oo son . . .
the dustbins?	**les poubelles?**
	leh poobel
the showers?	**les douches?**
	leh doosh
the toilets?	**les WC?**
	leh veh-seh
At what time must one . . .	**A quelle heure doit-on . . .**
	ah keller dwah-ton . . .
go to bed?	**se coucher?**
	ser coosheh
get up?	**se lever?**
	ser lerveh
Please, have you got . . .	**S'il vous plaît, avez-vous . . .**
	sil voo pleh ahveh-voo . . .
a broom?	**un balai?**
	an bah-leh
a corkscrew?	**un tire-bouchon?**
	an teer-booshon
a drying-up cloth?	**un torchon?**
	an torshon
a fork?	**une fourchette?**
	oon foorshet
a fridge?	**un frigo?**
	an freego
a frying pan?	**une poêle?**
	oon pwahl
an iron?	**un fer à repasser?**
	an fair ah rer-passeh
a knife?	**un couteau?**
	an cooto
a plate?	**une assiette?**
	oon ass-yet
a saucepan?	**une casserole?**
	oon cass-rol
a teaspoon?	**une cuillère à café**
	oon kwee-yeh ah cahfeh

Please, have you got . . .	**S'il vous plait, avez-vous . . .** sil voo pleh ahveh-voo . . .
a tin opener	**un ouvre-boîte?** an oov-bwaht
any washing powder?	**de la lessive?** der lah lesseeve
any washing-up liquid?	**du liquide pour la vaisselle?** doo leeked poor lah veh-sel
The bill, please	**La note, s'il vous plaît** lah not sil voo pleh

Problems

The toilet	**Le WC** ler veh-seh
The shower	**La douche** lah doosh
The tap	**Le robinet** ler robbeeneh
The razor point	**La prise pour le rasoir** lah preez poor ler rah-zwah
The light	**La lumiére** lah loom-yair
. . . is not working	**. . . ne marche pas** . . . ner marsh pah
My camping gas has run out	**Je n'ai plus de gaz** sher neh ploo der gaz

LIKELY REACTIONS

Have you an identity document?	**Avez-vous une pièce d'identité?** ahveh-voo oon pee-ess deedahnteeteh
Your membership card, please	**Votre carte, s'il vous plait** vot cart sil voo pleh
What's your name? [see p. 14.]	**Votre nom, s'il vous plaît** vot nom sil voo pleh
Sorry, we're full	**Je regrette, c'est complet** sher rer-gret seh compleh
How many people is it for?	**C'est pour combien de personnes?** seh poor combee-an der pairson

How many nights is it for? **C'est pour combien de nuits?**
seh poor combee-an der nwee

It's (5) francs . . . **C'est (cinq) francs . . .**
seh (san) frahn . . .

per day/per night **par jour/par nuit**
par shoor/par nwee

[*For numbers, see p. 126.*]

Rented accommodation: problem solving

ESSENTIAL INFORMATION

● If you're looking for accommodation to rent, look out for:

A LOUER	(to let)
APPARTEMENT	(flat)
CHALET	(part-timbered house)
FERME	(farmhouse)
MAISON	(house)
STUDIO	(flatlet)
VILLA	(detached house with garden)

● For arranging details of your let, see 'Hotel', p. 25.
● Key words you will meet if renting on the spot:
les arrhes (deposit)
lez-are
la clé (key)
lah cleh
● Having arranged your own accommodation and arrived with the key, check the obvious basics that you take for granted at home.
Electricity: Voltage? Razors and small appliances brought from home may need adjusting. You may need an adaptor.
Gas: Town gas or bottled gas? Butane gas must be kept indoors, propane gas must be kept outdoors.
Cooker: Don't be surprised to find:
the grill inside the oven, or no grill at all
a lid covering the rings which lifts up to form a 'splash-back'
a mixture of two gas rings and two electric rings.

Toilet: Mains drainage or septic tank? Don't flush disposable nappies or anything else down the toilet if you are on a septic tank.

Water: Find the stopcock. Check taps and plugs – they may not operate in the way you are used to. Check how to turn on (or light) the hot water.

Windows: Check the method of opening and closing windows and shutters.

Insects: Is an insecticide spray provided? If not, get one locally.

Equipment: For buying or replacing equipment, see p. 52.

● You will probably have an official agent, but be clear in your own mind who to contact in an emergency, even if it is only a neighbour in the first instance.

WHAT TO SAY

My name is . . .	**Je m'appelle . . .** shmappel . . .
I'm staying at . . .	**Je suis à . . .** sher swee ah . . .
They've cut off . . .	**On a coupé . . .** on ah coopeh . . .
the electricity	**l'électricité** leh-lectricit-eh
the gas	**le gaz** ler gaz
the water	**l'eau** lo
Is there . . . in the area?	**Est-ce qu'il y a . . . par ici** eskil yah . . . par ee-see
an electrician	**un électricien** an electri-see-an
a plumber	**un plombier** an plom-bee-eh
a gas fitter	**un employé du gaz** an ahmplwah-yeh doo gaz
Where is . . .	**Où est . . .** oo eh . . .
the fuse box?	**la boîte à fusibles?** lah bwaht ah foozeeb

the stopcock?	**le robinet d'arrêt?**
	ler robbeeneh dah-reh
the boiler?	**la chaudière?**
	lah shodee-air
the water heater?	**le chauffe-eau?**
	ler shof-o
Is there ...	**Est-ce qu'il y a ...**
	eskil yah ...
town gas?	**le gaz de ville?**
	ler gaz der veel
bottled gas?	**du gaz en bouteille?**
	doo gaz ahn bootay
a septic tank?	**une fosse septique?**
	oon foss septeek
central heating?	**le chauffage central?**
	ler shofash sahntrahl
The cooker	**La cuisinière**
	lah kweezeen-yair
The hair dryer	**Le séchoir à cheveux**
	ler seh-shwah ah sher-ver
The heating	**Le chauffage**
	ler shofash
The immersion heater	**Le chauffe-bains**
	ler shof-ban
The iron	**Le fer à repasser**
	ler fair ah rer-passeh
The pilot light	**La veilleuse**
	lah veh-yerz
The refrigerator	**Le réfrigérateur**
	ler refrisheh-rahter
The telephone	**Le téléphone**
	ler telefon
The toilet	**Le WC**
	ler veh-seh
The washing machine	**La machine à laver**
	lah machine ah lahveh
... is not working	**... ne marche pas**
	... ner marsh pah
Where can I get ...	**Où puis-je trouver ...**
	oo pweesh trooveh ...
an adaptor for this?	**un adaptateur pour ceci?**
	an ah-daptahter poor ser-see

Where can I get ...	**Où puis-je trouver ...**
	oo pweesh trooveh ...
a bottle of butane gas?	**une bouteille de gaz butane?**
	oon bootay der gaz boo-tan
a bottle of propane gas?	**une bouteille de gaz propane?**
	oon bootay der gaz pro-pan
a fuse?	**un fusible?**
	an foozeeb
an insecticide spray?	**une bombe insecticide?**
	oon bomb-ansectee-seed
a light bulb?	**une ampoule électrique?**
	oon ahmpool ehlectreek
The drain	**Le tuyau**
	ler twee-yo
The sink	**L'évier**
	lev-yeh
The toilet	**Le WC**
	ler veh-seh
... is blocked	**... est bouché**
	... eh boosheh
The gas is leaking	**Il y a une fuite de gaz**
	il ya oon fweet der gaz
Can you mend it straightaway?	**Pouvez-vous le réparer tout de suite?**
	pooveh-voo ler reh-pahreh too der sweet
When can you mend it?	**Quand pouvez-vous le réparer?**
	kahn pooveh-voo ler reh-pahreh
How much do I owe you?	**Combien vous dois-je?**
	combee-an voo dwah-sh
When is the rubbish collected?	**Quand ramasse-t-on les ordures?**
	kahn rahmass-ton leh zordoor

LIKELY REACTIONS

What's your name?	**Comment vous appelez-vous?**
	commahn voo zappleh-voo
What's your address?	**Quelle est votre adresse?**
	kel eh vot address
There's a shop ...	**Il y a un magasin ...**
	il yah an mahgahzan ...
in town/in the village	**en ville/dans le village**
	ahn veel/dahn ler veelash

I can't come ...	**Je ne peux pas venir ...**
	sher ner per pah ver-neer ...
today	**aujourd'hui**
	o-shoordwee
this week	**cette semaine**
	set ser-men
until Monday	**avant lundi**
	ahvahn lerndee
I can come ...	**Je peux venir ...**
	sher per ver-neer ...
on Tuesday	**mardi**
	mardee
when you want	**quand vous voulez**
	kahn voo vooleh
Every day	**Tous les jours**
	too leh shoor
Every other day	**Tous les deux jours**
	too leh der shoor
On Wednesdays	**Le mercredi**
	ler mairk-dee

[*For days of the week, see p. 130.*]

General shopping

The chemist's

ESSENTIAL INFORMATION

- Look for the word **PHARMACIE** or this sign.
- Medicines (drugs) are only available at a chemist's.
- Some non-drugs can be bought at a supermarket or department store, of course.
- Try the chemist *before* going to a doctor: they are usually qualified to treat minor injuries.
- To claim money back on prescriptions, remove price labels from medicines, and stick them on the prescription sheet.
- Chemists take it in turns to stay open all night and on Sundays. A notice on the door headed **PHARMACIE DE GARDE** or **PHARMACIE DE SERVICE** gives the address of the nearest chemist on duty.
- Some toiletries can also be bought at a **PARFUMERIE** but these will be more expensive.
- Finding a chemist, see p. 18.

WHAT TO SAY

I'd like . . .	Je voudrais . . .
	sher voodreh . . .
some Alka Seltzer	**de l'Alka Seltzer**
	der lalka seltzer
some antiseptic	**un antiseptique**
	an anti-septeek
some aspirin	**de l'aspirine**
	der laspeereen
some bandage	**une bande**
	oon bahnd

some cotton wool	**du coton**
	doo cotton
some eye drops	**des gouttes pour les yeux**
	deh goot poor leh zee-er
some foot powder	**une poudre anti-perspirante**
	oon pood anti-pairspeerahnt
some gauze dressing	**de la gaze**
	der lah gahz
some inhalant	**un inhalateur**
	an eenahlah-ter
some insect repellent	**une crème anti-moustiques**
	oon crem anti-moosteek
some lip salve	**de la pommade 'Rosa'**
	der lah pom-ad rozah
some nose drops	**des gouttes pour le nez**
	deh goot poor ler neh
some sticking plaster	**du sparadrap**
	doo spahrahdrah
some throat pastilles	**des pastilles pour la gorge**
	deh pass-tee poor lah gorsh
some Vaseline	**de la Vaseline**
	der lah vasleen
I'd like something for ...	**Je voudrais un produit pour ...**
	sher voodreh an prodwee poor ...
bites/stings (insect)	**les piqûres (d'insectes)**
	leh peek-oor (dan-sect)
burns/scalds	**les brûlures**
	leh brool-yoor
chilblains	**les engelures**
	leh zahn-sher-yoor
a cold	**le rhume**
	ler room
constipation	**la constipation**
	lah consteepah-see-on
a cough	**la toux**
	lah too
diarrhoea	**la diarrhée**
	lah dee-ah-reh
ear-ache	**le mal d'oreille**
	ler mal doray
flu	**la grippe**
	lah greep

I'd like something for ...	**Je voudrais un produit pour ...**
	sher voodreh an prodwee poor ...
sore gums	**la gingivite**
	lah shanshee-veet
sprains	**les entorses**
	leh zahntorss
sunburn	**les coups de soleil**
	leh coo der solay
travel sickness	**le mal de mer**
	ler mal der mair
I'd like ...	**Je voudrais ...**
	sher voodreh ...
some baby food	**de la nourriture pour bébés**
	der lah nooreetoor poor behbeh
some contraceptives	**des contraceptifs**
	deh contraceptif
some deodorant	**un déodorant**
	an deh-odorahn
some disposable nappies	**des couches en cellulose**
	deh coosh ahn celluloz
some handcream	**de la crème pour les mains**
	der lah crem poor leh man
some lipstick	**du rouge à lèvres**
	doo roosh ah lev
some make-up remover	**un démaquillant**
	an dehmahkee-yahn
some paper tissues	**des Kleenex**
	deh kleenex
some razor blades	**des lames de rasoir**
	deh lam der rahzwah
some safety pins	**des épingles de sûreté**
	dez ehpang der soor-teh
some sanitary towels	**des serviettes périodiques**
	deh sairv-yet pehree-odeek
some shaving cream	**de la crème à raser**
	der lah crem ah rahzeh
some soap	**du savon**
	doo sav-on
some suntan lotion/oil	**une crème/huile solaire**
	oon crem/weel solair

some talcum powder	**du talc**
	doo talc
some Tampax	**des Tampax**
	deh tampax
some toilet paper	**du papier hygiénique**
	doo pap-yeh eeshee-ehneek
some toothpaste	**du dentifrice**
	doo dahnteefreess

[*For other essential expressions, see 'Shop Talk', p. 54.*]

Holiday items

ESSENTIAL INFORMATION

- Places to shop at and signs to look for:
  LIBRAIRIE-PAPÈTERIE (stationer's)
  BUREAU DE TABAC (tobacconist's)
  CARTES POSTALES - SOUVENIRS (postcards - souvenirs)
  PHOTOGRAPHIE (films and photographic equipment)
- and the main department stores:
  MONOPRIX
  PRISUNIC
  INNO

WHAT TO SAY

Where can I buy . . . ?	**Où puis-je acheter . . . ?**
	oo pweesh ashteh . . .
I'd like . . .	**Je voudrais . . .**
	sher voodreh . . .
a bag	**un sac**
	an sac
a beach ball	**un ballon pour la plage**
	an bah-lon poor lah plash
a bucket	**un seau**
	an so
an English newspaper	**un journal anglais**
	an shoornahl ahngleh
some envelopes	**des enveloppes**
	deh zahnv-lop
a guide book	**un guide**
	an gheed
a map (of the area)	**une carte (de la région)**
	oon cart (der lah resh-yon)
some postcards	**des cartes postales**
	deh cart postahl
a spade	**une pelle**
	oon pel
a straw hat	**un chapeau de paille**
	an shahpo der pie

a suitcase	**une valise**
	oon val-eez
some sunglasses	**des lunettes de soleil**
	deh loonet der solay
a sunshade	**un parasol**
	an parasol
an umbrella	**un parapluie**
	an para-plwee
some writing paper	**du papier à lettres**
	doo pap-yeh ah let
I'd like . . . [*show the camera*]	**Je voudrais . . .**
	sher voodreh . . .
a colour film	**un rouleau de pellicules couleur**
	an roolo der pelleecool cooler
a black and white film	**un rouleau de pellicules noir et blanc**
	an roolo der pelleecool nwah eh blahn
for prints	**pour photos**
	poor photo
for slides	**pour diapositives**
	poor dee-ah-positive
12 (24/36) exposures	**douze (vingt-quatre/trente-six) poses**
	dooz (vant-cat/trahnt-see) pose
a standard 8 mm film	**un film ordinaire huit millimètres**
	an film ordeenair wee meeleemet
a super 8 film	**un film super huit**
	an film soopair weet
some flash bulbs	**des flash**
	deh flash
This camera is broken	**Cet appareil ne marche plus**
	set appahray ner marsh ploo
The film is stuck	**Le film est coincé**
	ler film eh kwen-seh
Please can you . . .	**S'il vous plaît, pouvez-vous . . .**
	sil voo pleh pooveh-voo . . .
develop/print this?	**développer/tirer ceci?**
	dev-loppeh/tee-reh ser-see
load the camera for me?	**charger l'appareil?**
	shar-sheh lappahray

[*For other essential expressions, see 'Shop talk', p. 54.*]

The tobacconist's

ESSENTIAL INFORMATION

- Tobacco is sold only where you see these signs.
- A tobacconist's is called a **BUREAU DE TABAC**.
- See p. 18 to ask if there is one near by.
- Tobacconists always sell postage stamps.
- A tobacconist's is sometimes part of a café (**CAFÉ-TABAC**), a stationer's (**PAPÈTERIE**) or newsagent (**TABAC-JOURNAUX**).

WHAT TO SAY

A packet of cigarettes . . .   **Un paquet de cigarettes . . .**
an pak-eh der cigarette . . .

   with filters   **à bout filtre**
ah boo feelt

   without filters   **sans filtre**
sahn feelt

   king size   **longues**
long

   menthol   **à la menthe**
ah lah mahnt

Those up there . . .   **Celles-là, en haut . . .**
cell-lah ahn o . . .

   on the right   **à droite**
ah drwaht

   on the left   **à gauche**
ah goshe

These [*point*]	**Celles-ci**
	cell-see
Cigarettes, please	**Des cigarettes, s'il vous plaît ...**
	deh cigarette, sil voo pleh ...
100, 200, 300	**cent, deux cents, trois cents**
	sahn, der sahn, trwah sahn
Two packets	**Deux paquets**
	der pak-eh
Have you got ...	**Avez-vous ...**
	ahveh-voo ...
English cigarettes?	**des cigarettes anglaises?**
	deh cigarette ahnglez
American cigarettes?	**des cigarettes américaines?**
	deh cigarette ameriken
English pipe tobacco?	**du tabac de pipe anglais?**
	doo tahbah der peep ahngleh
American pipe tobacco?	**du tabac de pipe américain?**
	doo tahbah der peep american
rolling tobacco?	**du tabac à rouler?**
	doo tahbah ah rooleh
A packet of pipe tobacco	**Un paquet de tabac de pipe**
	an pak-eh der tahbah der peep
That one down there ...	**Celui-là, en bas ...**
	ser-lwee-lah ahn bah ...
on the right	**à droite**
	ah drwaht
on the left	**à gauche**
	ah goshe
This one [*point*]	**Celui-ci**
	ser-lwee-see
A cigar, please	**Un cigare, s'il vous plaît**
	an cigar sil voo pleh
That one [*point*]	**Celui-là**
	ser-lwee-lah
Some cigars	**Des cigares**
	deh cigar
Those [*point*]	**Ceux-là**
	ser-lah
A box of matches	**Une boîte d'allumettes**
	oon bwaht dalloomet
A packet of pipe-cleaners	**Un paquet de cure-pipes**
	an pak-eh der cooer peep

A packet of flints	**Un paquet de pierres**
[show lighter]	an pak-eh der pee-air
Lighter fuel	**De l'essence à briquet**
	der lessahns ah breekeh
Lighter gas, please	**Du gaz pour briquet, s'il vous plaît**
	doo gaz poor breekeh sil voo pleh

[For other essential expressions, see 'Shop Talk', p. 54.]

Buying clothes

ESSENTIAL INFORMATION

● Look for:
  CONFECTION DAMES (women's clothes)
  CONFECTION HOMMES (men's clothes)
  CHAUSSURES (shoes)
● Don't buy without being measured first or without trying things on.
● Don't rely on coversion charts of clothing sizes [see p. 141].
● If you are buying for someone else, take their measurements with you (in centimetres).
● The department stores **MONOPRIX** and **PRISUNIC** sell clothes and shoes.

WHAT TO SAY

I'd like ...	**Je voudrais ...**
	sher voodreh ...
an anorak	**un anorak**
	an anorak
a belt	**une ceinture**
	oon centoor
a bikini	**un bikini**
	an bikini

a blouse	**un chemisier**
	an sher-meez-yeh
a bra	**un soutien-gorge**
	an soot-yen-gorsh
some briefs (women)	**une culotte**
	oon coolot
a cap (swimming/skiing)	**un bonnet (de bain/de ski)**
	an bonneh (der ban/der skee)
a cardigan	**un cardigan**
	an cardeegahn
a coat	**un manteau**
	an mahnto
a dress	**une robe**
	oon rob
a hat	**un chapeau**
	an shahpo
a jacket	**une veste**
	oon vest
some jeans	**un jean**
	an jean
a jumper/pullover	**un pullover**
	an poolovair
a nightdress	**une chemise de nuit**
	oon sher-meez der nwee
some pyjamas	**un pyjama**
	an peeshah-mah
a raincoat	**un imperméable**
	an ampair-meh-ab
a shirt (man's)	**une chemise**
	oon sher-meez
some shorts	**un short**
	an short
a skirt	**une jupe**
	oon shoop
a suit (man's)	**un costume**
	an costoom
a suit (woman's)	**un ensemble**
	an ahn-sahmb
a swimsuit	**un maillot de bain**
	an mah-yo der ban
some tights	**un collant**
	an collahn

I'd like . . .	**Je voudrais . . .**
	sher voodreh
some trousers	**un pantalon**
	an pahntah-lon
a T-shirt	**un tee-shirt**
	an tee-shirt
some underpants (men)	**un slip**
	an sleep
I'd like a pair of . . .	**Je voudrais une paire de . . .**
	sher voodreh oon pair der . . .
gloves	**gants**
	gahn
socks	**chaussettes**
	sho-set
stockings	**bas**
	bah
I'd like a pair of . . .	**Je voudrais une paire de . . .**
	sher voodreh oon pair der . . .
shoes	**chaussures**
	sho-sooer
canvas shoes	**chaussures en toile**
	sho-sooer ahn twahl
sandals	**sandales**
	sahndahl
beach shoes	**nu-pieds**
	noo pee-eh
smart shoes	**chaussures habillées**
	sho-sooer ahbee-yeh
boots	**bottes**
	bot
mocassins	**mocassins**
	mo-cah-san
My size is . . .	**Je prends du . . .**
[*For numbers, see p. 126*]	sher prahn doo . . .
Can you measure me, please?	**Pouvez-vous me mesurer, s'il vous plaît?**
	pooveh-voo mer mer-zoo-reh sil voo pleh
Can I try it on?	**Puis-je l'essayer?**
	pweesh lesseh-yeh
It's for a present	**C'est pour un cadeau**
	seh poor an cahdo

These are the measurements [*Show written*]	**Voici les mesures** vwah-see leh mer-zooer
bust/chest	**poitrine** pwahtreen
collar	**tour de cou** toor der coo
hips	**hanches** ahnsh
leg	**jambe** shahmb
shoulders	**épaules** ehpol
waist	**taille** tie
Have you got something . . .	**Avez-vous quelque chose . . .** ahveh-voo kelk shoz . . .
in black?	**en noir?** ahn nwah
in white?	**en blanc?** ahn blahn
in grey?	**en gris?** ahn gree
in blue?	**en bleu?** ahn bler
in brown?	**en marron?** ahn mah-ron
in pink?	**en rose?** ahn rose
in green	**en vert?** ahn vair
in red?	**en rouge?** ahn roosh
in yellow?	**en jaune?** ahn shon
in this colour [*point*]	**de cette couleur?** der set cooler
in cotton?	**en coton?** ahn cot-on
in denim?	**en toile?** ahn twahl
in leather?	**en cuir?** ahn kweer

Have you got something . . .	Avez-vous quelque chose . . .
	ahveh-voo kelk shoz . . .
in nylon?	**en nylon?**
	ahn neelon
in suede?	**en daim?**
	ahn dan
in wool?	**en laine?**
	ahn len
in this material? [*point*]	**dans ce tissu?**
	dahn ser tee-soo

[*For other essential expressions, see 'Shop talk', p. 54.*]

Replacing equipment

ESSENTIAL INFORMATION

- Look out for these shops and signs:
  QUINCAILLERIE   (hardware)
  ÉLECTRO-MÉNAGER   (electrical goods)
  DROGUERIE   (household cleaning materials)
- In a supermarket, look for this display: **ENTRETIEN**
- To ask the way to the shop, see p. 18.
- At a campsite try their shop first.

WHAT TO SAY

Have you got . . .	Avez-vous . . .
	ahveh-voo . . .
an adaptor? [*show appliance*]	**un adaptateur?**
	an ahdap-tahter
a bottle of butane gas?	**une bouteille de gaz butane?**
	oon bootay der gaz boo-tan
a bottle of propane gas?	**une bouteille de propane?**
	oon bootay der pro-pan
a bottle opener?	**un ouvre-bouteille?**
	an oov-bootay

a corkscrew?	**un tire-bouchon?**
	an teer-booshon
any disinfectant?	**un désinfectant?**
	an deh-zanfectahn
any disposable cups?	**des gobelets à jeter?**
	deh gob-leh ah sheteh
any disposable plates?	**des assiettes à jeter?**
	dez ass-yet ah sheteh
a drying-up cloth?	**un torchon?**
	an torshon
any forks?	**des fourchettes?**
	deh foorshet
a fuse? [*show old one*]	**un fusible?**
	an foozeeb
an insecticide spray?	**une bombe insecticide?**
	oon bomb-ansectee-seed
a paper kitchen roll?	**du sopalin?**
	doo sopahlan
any knives?	**des couteaux?**
	deh cooto
a light bulb? [*show old one*]	**une ampoule?**
	oon ahmpool
a plastic bucket?	**un seau en plastique?**
	an so ahn plasteek
a scouring pad?	**un tampon pour récurer?**
	an tahmpon poor reh-cooreh
a spanner?	**une clé plate?**
	oon cleh plat
a sponge?	**une éponge?**
	oon ehponsh
any string?	**de la ficelle?**
	der lah feecell
any tent pegs?	**des piquets de tente?**
	deh peekeh der tahnt
a tin opener?	**un ouvre-boîte?**
	an oov-bwaht
a torch?	**une lampe de poche?**
	oon lahmp der posh
any torch batteries?	**des piles pour lampe électrique?**
	deh peel poor lahmp electreek
a universal plug (for the sink)?	**un tampon universel (pour évier)?**
	an tahmpon ooneevair-sel (poor ev-yeh)

Have you got ...	**Avez-vous ...**
	ahveh-voo ...
a washing line?	**une corde à linge?**
	oon cord ah lansh
any washing powder?	**de la lessive?**
	der lah lesseeve
any washing-up liquid?	**du liquide pour la vaisselle?**
	doo leekeed poor lah veh-sell
a washing-up brush?	**une brosse pour la vaisselle?**
	oon bross poor lah veh-sell

[*For other essential expressions, see 'Shop talk', below.*]

Shop talk

ESSENTIAL INFORMATION

- Know your coins and notes: coins: see illustration.
  notes: 10F, 50F, 100F, 500F
  [*For numbers, see p. 126.*]
- Know how to say the important weights and measures:

50 grams	**cinquante grammes**
	sankahnt gram
100 grams	**cent grammes**
	sahn gram
200 grams	**deux cents grammes**
	der sahn gram
½ kilo	**un demi-kilo**
	an der-me keelo
1 kilo	**un kilo**
	an keelo
2 kilos	**deux kilos**
	der keelo
½ litre	**un demi-litre**
	an der-me leet
1 litre	**un litre**
	an leet
2 litres	**deux litres**
	der leet

● In small shops don't be surprised if customers, as well as the shop assistant, say 'hello' and 'goodbye' to you.

CUSTOMER

Hello ⎤	**Bonjour**
Good morning ⎦	bonshoor
Goodbye	**Au revoir**
	o-revwah
I'm just looking	**Je regarde**
	sher rer-gard
Excuse me	**Pardon**
	par-don
How much is this/that?	**C'est combien ça?**
	seh combee-an sah
What is that/what are those?	**Qu'est-ce que c'est ça?**
	kesk seh sah
Is there a discount?	**Est-ce que vous faites une remise?**
	esk voo fet oon rer-meez
I'd like that, please	**Je voudrais ça, s'il vous plaît**
	sher voodreh sah sil voo pleh
Not that	**Pas ça**
	pah sah
Like that	**Comme ça**
	com sah
That's enough, thank you	**Ça suffit, merci**
	sah soofee mair-see
More please	**Encore un peu, s'il vous plaît**
	ahncor an per sil voo pleh
Less please	**Moins, s'il vous plaît**
	mwen sil voo pleh
That's fine ⎤	**Ça va**
OK ⎦	sah vah
I won't take it, thank you	**Merci je ne le prends pas**
	mair-see sher ner ler prahn pah
It's not right	**Ça ne va pas**
	sah ner vah pah
Thank you very much	**Merci bien**
	mair-see bee-an

Have you got something . . .	**Avez-vous quelque chose . . .**
	ahveh-voo kelk shoz . . .
better?	**de mieux?**
	dee me-er
cheaper?	**de moins cher?**
	der mwen shair
different?	**de différent?**
	der dee-fay-rahn
larger?	**de plus grand?**
	der ploo grahn
smaller?	**de plus petit?**
	der ploo ptee
At what time do you . . .	**A quelle heure . . .**
	ah keller . . .
open?	**ouvrez-vous?**
	oovreh-voo
close?	**fermez-vous?**
	fairmeh-voo
Can I have a bag, please?	**Puis-je avoir un sac, s'il vous plaît?**
	Pweesh ahvwah an sac sil voo pleh
Can I have a receipt?	**Puis-je avoir un reçu?**
	pweesh ahvwah an rer-soo
Do you take . . .	**Acceptez-vous . . .**
	accepteh-voo . . .
English/American money?	**l'argent anglais/américain?**
	larshahn ahngleh/american
travellers' cheques?	**les traveller chèques?**
	leh traveller sheck
credit cards?	**la carte bleue?**
	lah cart bler
I'd like . . .	**J'en voudrais . . .**
	shahn voodreh . . .
one like that	**un comme ça**
	an com sah
two like that	**deux comme ça**
	der com sah

SHOP ASSISTANT

Can I help you?	**Qu'y a-t-il pour votre service?**
	kee ah-til poor vot sairvees
What would you like?	**Vous désirez?**
	voo dehzeereh
Will that be all?	**Ce sera tout?**
	ser ser-rah too
Is that all?	**C'est tout?**
	seh too
Anything else?	**Vous désirez autre chose?**
	voo dehzeereh ot shoz
Would you like it wrapped?	**Je vous l'enveloppe?**
	sher voo lahnv-lop
Sorry, none left	**Je regrette, il n'y en a plus**
	sher rer-gret il nee ahn-nah ploo
I haven't got any	**Je n'en ai pas**
	sher nahn-neh pah
I haven't got any more	**Je n'en ai plus**
	sher nahn-neh ploo
How many do you want? ⎤	**Vous en voulez combien?**
How much do you want? ⎦	voo-zahn vooleh combee-an
Is that enough?	**Ça suffit?**
	sah soofee

Shopping for food

Bread

ESSENTIAL INFORMATION

- Finding a bakers, see p. 19.
- Key words to look for:
  BOULANGERIE (baker's)
  BOULANGER (baker)
  PAIN (bread)
- Hypermarkets, supermarkets of any size and general stores nearly always sell bread.
- Small bakers are usually open between 7.30 a.m. and 7/8 p.m. Most close on Mondays and public holidays but open on Sunday mornings.
- The most characteristic kind of loaf is the 'French stick', which comes in a number of sizes.
- For any other type of loaf, say **'un pain'** (an pan) and point.

WHAT TO SAY

Some bread, please	**Du pain, s'il vous plaît** doo pan sil voo pleh
A loaf (like that)	**Un pain (comme ça)** an pan (com sah)
A French stick	**Une baguette** oon bah-get
A large one	**Une grande** oon grahnd
A long, thin one	**Une ficelle** oon feesel
Half a French stick	**Une demi-baguette** oon der-me bah-get
A brown loaf	**Un pain intégral** an pan an-tay-gral
A bread roll	**Un petit pain** an ptee pan

A crescent roll	**Un croissant**
	an crwah-sahn
A small milk loaf bun	**Une brioche**
	oon bree-osh
A small sweet bun with sultanas	**Un pain aux raisins**
	an pan o rehzan
A small bun of brioche texture with dark chocolate filling	**Un pain au chocolat**
	an pan o shocolah
Two loaves	**Deux pains**
	der pan
Two French sticks	**Deux baguettes**
	der bah-get
Four bread rolls	**Quatre petits pains**
	kat ptee pan
Four crescent rolls	**Quatre croissants**
	kat crwah-sahn

[*For other essential expressions, see 'Shop talk', p. 54.*]

Cakes

ESSENTIAL INFORMATION

- Key words to look for:
  PÂTISSERIE   (cake shop)
  PÂTISSIER   (cake/pastry maker)
  PÂTISSERIES   (pastries/cakes)
- To find a cake shop, see p. 18.
- **SALON DE THÉ**: a room, usually off a pâtisserie, where customers sit at tables and are served with cakes, ices, soft drinks, tea, coffee or chocolate. See p. 80, 'Ordering a drink'.
- Pâtisseries are open on Sundays, but not on Mondays.

WHAT TO SAY

The types of cakes you find in the shops vary from region to region, but the following are some of the most common.

un éclair	an eclair
an eclair	
un chou à la crème	choux pastry filled with vanilla
an shoo ah lah crem	cream
une religieuse	choux pastry in the shape of a small
oon rer-leeshee-erz	cottage loaf with coffee cream filling (literally: a nun)
un baba au rhum	a rum baba
an bahbah o rom	
un millefeuille	alternate layers of puff pastry and
an meelfey	almond cream
un chausson aux pommes	an apple turnover
an sho-son o pom	
un pet de nonne	a doughnut
an peh der non	
une tartelette aux pommes	a small apple tart
oon tartlet o pom	
... aux fraises	... strawberry
... o frez	
... aux abricots	... apricot
.. o-zahbreeco	

You usually buy medium-size cakes by number:

Two doughnuts, please
Deux pets de nonne, s'il vous plaît
der peh der non, sil voo pleh

Half a dozen cream cakes
Une demi-douzaine de gâteaux à la crème
oon der-me doozen der gahto ah lah crem

You buy small cakes by weight:

200 grams of petits fours
Deux cents grammes de petits fours
der sahn gram der ptee foor

400 grams of biscuits
Quatre cents grammes de biscuits
kat sahn gram der bee-skwee

You may want to buy a larger cake by the slice:

One slice of apple cake
Une tranche de gâteau aux pommes
oon trahnsh der gahto o pom

Two slices of almond cake
Deux tranches de gâteau aux amandes
der trahnsh der gahto o-zahmahnd

You may also want to say:

A selection, please
Mélangés, s'il vous plaît
mel-ahnsheh sil voo pleh

[*For other essential expressions, see 'Shop talk', p. 54.*]

Ice-cream and sweets

ESSENTIAL INFORMATION

- Key words to look for:
GLACES	(ice-creams)
GLACIER	(ice-cream maker/seller)
CONFISERIE	(sweet shop)
CONFISEUR	(sweet maker/seller)
PÂTISSIER	(cake/pastry maker)
- Best known ice-cream brand names are:
FRIGÉCRÈME	**MOTTA**
GERVAIS	**SKI**
MIKO	
- Prepacked sweets are available in general stores and supermarkets.

WHAT TO SAY

A ... ice, please	**Une glace ... s'il vous plaît**
	oon glass ... sil voo pleh
banana	**à la banane**
	ah lah bah-nan
chocolate	**au chocolat**
	o shocolah
coffee	**au moka**
	o mokah
pistachio	**à la pistache**
	ah lah pee-stash
raspberry	**à la framboise**
	ah lah frahm-bwahz
strawberry	**à la fraise**
	ah lah frez
vanilla	**à la vanille**
	ah lah vahneel
Two francs worth	**Deux francs**
	der frahn
A single cone [*specify flavour, as above*]	**Un cornet simple**
	an corneh samp

Two single cones	**Deux cornets simples**
	der corneh samp
A double cone	**Un cornet double**
	an corneh doob
Two double cones	**Deux cornets doubles**
	der corneh doob
A mixed cone [*specify flavours, as above*]	**Un cornet mélangé**
	an corneh mel-ahnsheh
A tub	**Un carton**
	an carton
A lollipop	**Une sucette**
	oon soo-set
A packet of ...	**Un paquet de ...**
	an pak-eh der ...
100 grams of ...	**Cent grammes de ...**
	sahn gram der ...
200 grams of ...	**Deux cents grammes de ...**
	der sahn gram der ...
sweets	**bonbons**
	bonbon
toffees	**caramels**
	caramel
chocolates	**chocolats**
	shocolah
mints	**bonbons à la menthe**
	bonbon ah lah mahnt

[*For other essential expressions, see 'Shop talk', p. 54.*]

In the supermarket

ESSENTIAL INFORMATION

- The place to ask for: [see p. 18]

UN SUPERMARCHÉ	(supermarket)
UN HYPERMARCHÉ	(hypermarket)
UNE SUPERETTE	(corner self-service)
UNE ALIMENTATION GÉNÉRALE	(general food store)

- Key instructions on signs in the shop:

ENTRÉE	(entrance)
ENTRÉE INTERDITE	(no entry)
SORTIE	(exit)
SORTIE INTERDITE	(no exit)
SANS ISSUE	(no way out)
SORTIE SANS ACHATS	(exit for non-buyers)
CAISSE	(check-out, cash desk)
CAISSE RAPIDE	(check-out for 6 items or less)
EN RÉCLAME	(on offer)
LIBRE SERVICE	(self-service)
CHARIOTS	(trolleys)

- Opening times vary but most shops are open between 8 a.m. and 7 p.m. Hypermarkets will often remain open until 10 p.m. Remember, however, that the majority of shops are closed on Mondays.
- No need to say anything in a supermarket, but ask if you can't see what you want.
- For non-food items, see 'Replacing equipment', p. 48.

WHAT TO SAY

Excuse me, please	**Pardonnez-moi, s'il vous plaît**
	par-don-neh mwah sil voo pleh
Where is . . .	**Où est . . .**
	oo eh . . .
the bread?	**le pain?**
	ler pan
the butter?	**le beurre?**
	ler bər

Where is . . .	**Où est . . .**
	oo eh . . .
the cheese?	**le fromage?**
	ler fromash
the chocolate?	**le chocolat?**
	ler shocolah
the coffee?	**le café?**
	ler cahfeh
the cooking oil?	**l'huile?**
	lweel
the fish (fresh)?	**le poisson?**
	ler pwah-son
the jam?	**la confiture?**
	lah confeetoor
the meat?	**la viande?**
	la vee-ahnd
the milk?	**le lait?**
	ler leh
the mineral water?	**l'eau minérale?**
	lo mee-nehrahl
the salt?	**le sel?**
	ler sel
the sugar?	**le sucre?**
	ler sook
the tea?	**le thé?**
	ler teh
the tinned fish?	**le poisson en conserve?**
	ler pwah-son ahn con-sairv
the vinegar?	**le vinaigre?**
	ler vee-neg
the wine?	**le vin?**
	ler van
Where are . . .	**Où sont . . .**
	oo son . . .
the biscuits?	**les biscuits?**
	leh biskwee
the crisps?	**les pommes chips?**
	leh pom ship
the eggs?	**les œufs?**
	leh zer
the frozen foods?	**les produits surgelés?**
	leh prodwee soorsh-leh

the fruit juices?	**les jus de fruits?**
	leh shoo der frwee
the pastas?	**les pâtes?**
	leh pat
the seafoods?	**les fruits de mer?**
	leh frwee der mair
the snails? .	**les escargots?**
	leh zescargo
the soft drinks?	**les boissons?**
	leh bwah-son
the sweets?	**les bonbons?**
	leh bonbon
the tinned vegetables?	**les légumes en conserve?**
	leh lehgoom ahn con-sairv
the vegetables?	**les légumes?**
	leh lehgoom
Where is . . .	**Où sont . . .**
	oo son . . .
the fruit?	**les fruits?**
	leh frwee
the tinned fruit?	**les fruits en conserve?**
	leh frwee ahn con-sairv
the yogurt?	**les yaourts?**
	leh yah-oor

[*For other essential expressions, see 'Shop talk', p. 54.*]

Picnic food

ESSENTIAL INFORMATION

- Key words to look for:
CHARCUTERIE	(pork butcher's, delicatessen)
TRAITEUR	(delicatessen)
CHARCUTIER	(pork butcher)
- In these shops you can buy a wide variety of food such as ham, salami, cheese, olives, appetizers, sausages and freshly made takeaway dishes. Specialities differ from region to region.
- Weight guide:
  4–6 oz/150 g of prepared salad per two people, if eaten as a starter to a substantial meal.
  3–4 oz/100 g of prepared salad per person, if eaten at the main part of a picnic-type meal.

WHAT TO SAY

A slice of ...	**Une tranche de ...**
	oon trahnsh der ...
Two slices of ...	**Deux tranches de ...**
	der trahnsh der ...
garlic sausage	**saucisson à l'ail**
	so-see-son ah lie
ham (cooked)	**jambon cuit**
	shahmbon kwee
ham (cured)	**jambon cru**
	shahmbon croo
pâté	**pâté**
	pahteh
roast beef	**rôti de bœuf**
	rotee der berf
roast pork	**rôti de porc**
	rotee der por
salami	**saucisson**
	so-see-son
100 grams of ...	**Cent grammes de* ...**
	sahn gram der ...

150 grams of . . .	**Cent cinquante grammes de* . . .**
	sahn sankahnt gram der . . .
200 grams of . . .	**Deux cents grammes de* . . .**
	der sahn gram der . . .
300 grams of . . .	**Trois cents grammes de* . . .**
	trwah sahn gram der . . .
Russian salad	**salade russe**
	sal-ad rooss
tomato salad	**salade de tomates**
	sal-ad der tomaht
olives	**olives**
	oleev
anchovies	**anchois**
	ahn-shwah
cheese	**fromage**
	fromash

* Use **d'** in front of words beginning with a vowel.

You might also like to try some of these:

andouille	tripe sausage
ahn-dooy	
barquette de crevettes	boat-shaped pastry case with prawn
barket der crer-vet	filling
bœuf aux champignons	diced beef cooked with wine and
berf o shahmpeen-yon	mushrooms
. . . aux olives	sliced beef cooked with wine and
. . . o zoleev	olives
. . . en daube	diced beef in a thick wine sauce
. . . ahn dobe	
bouchée à la reine	vol-au-vent case filled with sweet-
boo-shay ah lah rain	breads and mushrooms in cream
	sauce
boudin	black pudding
boo-dain	
brandade de morue	salt cod, crushed and mixed with
brahn-dad der moroo	oil, cream and garlic
champignons à la grecque	mushrooms cooked in wine,
shahmpeen-yon ah lah grec	tomatoes and spices
cœurs d'artichaux	artichoke hearts
ker dar-tee-sho	

macédoine de légumes masshe-dwan der lehgoom	diced vegetables in mayonnaise
œufs mayonnaise er my-onez	hard boiled eggs with mayonnaise
quiche lorraine keesh lorren	egg and ham/bacon pie
rillettes ree-yet	minced pork (goose or duck) baked in fat
rouleau au fromage roolo o fromash	pastry roll with creamy cheese filling
salade niçoise sal-ad nee-swahz	tomato, potato, egg, anchovy, tunny fish and olive salad in oil and vinegar
saucisse de Strasbourg so-seess der strasboor	frankfurter
saucisson sec so-see-son sec	smoked garlic sausage
tarte à l'oignon tart ah lonion	onion pie
tarte au fromage tart o fromash	cheese pie
tomates farcies tomaht far-see	stuffed tomatoes
Brie bree	creamy white cheese
Camembert cahmahmbair	full fat soft white cheese
Emmental emmentahl	Swiss cheese with big holes
fromage de chèvre fromash der shev	goat's cheese
Gruyère gru-yair	Swiss cheese, rich in flavour, smooth in texture
Pont l'Évêque pon leh-vek	soft, runny cheese with holes, strong flavour
Roquefort rockfor	resembles Stilton

[*For other essential expressions, see 'Shop talk', p. 54.*]

Fruit and vegetables

ESSENTIAL INFORMATION

● Key words to look for:
FRUITS	(fruit)
LÉGUMES	(vegetables)
PRIMEURS	(fresh fruit and vegetables)
FRUITIER	(fruit seller)
MARCHÉ	(market)

● If possible, buy fruit and vegetables in the market where they are cheaper and fresher than in the shops. Open-air markets are held once or twice a week in most areas (or daily in large towns), usually in the mornings.

● It is customary for you to choose your own fruit and vegetables at the market (and in some shops) and for the stallholder to weigh and price them. You must take your own shopping bag: paper and plastic bags are not normally provided.

● Weight guide: 1 kg of potatoes is sufficient for six people for one meal.

WHAT TO SAY

½ kilo (1 lb) of ...	**Un demi-kilo de*** ...
	an der-me keelo der ...
1 kilo of ...	**Un kilo de*** ...
	an keelo der ...
2 kilos of ...	**Deux kilos de*** ...
	der keelo der ...
apples	**pommes**
	pom
bananas	**bananes**
	bah-nan
cherries	**cerises**
	ser-eez
grapes (white/black)	**raisins (blancs/noirs)**
	rehzan (blahn/nwah)
oranges	**oranges**
	orahnsh

2 kilos of ...	**Deux kilos de* ...**
	der keelo der ...
peaches	**pêches**
	pesh
pears	**poires**
	pwah
plums	**prunes**
	proon
strawberries	**fraises**
	frez
A grapefruit, please	**Un pamplemousse, s'il vous plaît**
	an pahmp-mousse sil voo pleh
A melon	**Un melon**
	an mer-lon
A pineapple	**Un ananas**
	an ahnahnah
A water melon	**Une pastèque**
	oon passtek
250 grams of ...	**Deux cents cinquante grammes de*...**
	der sahn sankahnt gram der ...
½ kilo of ...	**Un demi-kilo de* ...**
	an der-me keelo der ...
1 kilo of ...	**Un kilo de* ...**
	an keelo der ...
1½ kilos of ...	**Un kilo et demi de* ...**
	an keelo eh der-me der ...
2 kilos of ...	**Deux kilos de* ...**
	der keelo der ...
asparagus	**asperges**
	aspersh
carrots	**carottes**
	car-rot
green beans	**haricots verts**
	ahreeco vair
leeks	**poireaux**
	pwah-ro
mushrooms	**champignons**
	shahmpeen-yon
onions	**oignons**
	onion
peas	**petits pois**
	ptee pwah

* Use **d'** in front of words beginning with a vowel.

peppers (green/red)	**poivrons (verts/rouges)**
	pwah-vron (vair/roosh)
potatoes	**pommes de terre**
	pom der tair
shallots	**échalotes**
	eh-shallot
spinach	**épinards**
	ehpeenar
tomatoes	**tomates**
	tomaht
A bunch of parsley	**Un bouquet de persil**
	an bookeh der pair-see
A bunch of radishes	**Une botte de radis**
	oon bot der rahdee
A head of garlic	**Une tête d'ail**
	oon tet die
A lettuce	**Une salade**
	oon sal-ad
A cauliflower	**Un chou-fleur**
	an shoo-fler
A cabbage	**Un chou**
	an shoo
A stick of celery	**Un pied de céleri**
	an pee-eh der seleree
A cucumber	**Un concombre**
	an concomb
Like that, please	**Comme ça, s'il vous plaît**
	com sah sil voo pleh

These are some vegetables which may not be familiar:

aubergines	egg-plants – purple and shiny
obairsheen	
blettes	sea-kale
blet	
courgettes	very small marrows
coorshet	
fenouil	fennels – crunchy vegetables with
fer-nooy	aniseed flavour

For other essential expressions, see 'Shop talk', p. 54.]

Meat

ESSENTIAL INFORMATION

- Key words to look for:
  BOUCHERIE   (butcher's)
  BOUCHER   (butcher)
- Weight guide: 4–6 oz/125–200 g of meat per person for one meal.
- The diagrams opposite are to help you make sense of labels on counters and supermarket displays, and decide which cut or joint to have. Translations do not help, and you don't need to say the French word involved.

WHAT TO SAY

For a joint, choose the type of meat and then say how many people it is for:

Some beef, please	**Du bœuf, s'il vous plaît** doo berf sil voo pleh
Some lamb	**De l'agneau** der lan-yo
Some mutton	**Du mouton** doo mooton
Some pork	**Du porc** doo por
Some veal	**Du veau** doo vo
A joint ...	**Un rôti ...** an rotee ...
for two people	**pour deux personnes** poor der pair-son
for four people	**pour quatre personnes** poor kat pair-son
for six people	**pour six personnes** poor see pair-son

Beef Bœuf

1 Aiguillette baronne
2 Romsteck
3 Tranche grasse
4 Gîte à la noix
5 Gîte-gîte
6 Bavette (pot-au-feu)
7 Contre-filet
8 Entrecôtes   13 Second talon
9 Paleron   14 Veine grasse
10 Flanchet   15 Macreuse
11 Tendron   16 Poitrine
12 Plat de côtes   17 Gîte-gîte

Veal Veau

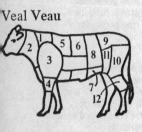

1 Côtes découvertes
2 Collier
3 Epaule
4 Jarret de devant
5 Côtes secondes
6 Côtes premières
7 Flanchet
8 Longe
9 Quasi   11 Noix pâtissière
10 Sous-noix   12 Jarret

Pork Porc

1 Filet
2 Pointe
3 Jambon
4 Ventre
5 Côtes premières
6 Côtes découvertes
7 Echine
8 Tête   10 Jambonneau
9 Epaule   11 Poitrine

Lamb Mouton

1 Côtes premières
2 Selle
3 Filet
4 Gigot
5 Haut de côtelettes
6 Côtes secondes
7 Côtes découvertes
8 Collier
9 Epaule   10 Poitrine

For steak, liver or kidneys, do as above:

Some steak, please	**Du biftek, s'il vous plaît** doo beeftek sil voo pleh
Some liver	**Du foie** doo fwah
Some kidneys	**Des rognons** deh ron-yon
Some heart	**Du cœur** doo ker
Some sausages	**Des saucisses** deh so-seess
Some mince . . .	**De la viande hachée** der lah vee-ahnd asheh
for three people	**pour trois personnes** poor trawh pair-son
for five people	**pour cinq personnes** poor san pair-son

For chops do it this way:

Two veal escalopes	**Deux escalopes de veau** der escalop der vo
Three pork chops	**Trois côtelettes de porc** trwah cotlet der por
Four lamb chops	**Quatre côtelettes d'agneau** kat cotlet dan-yo
Five mutton chops	**Cinq côtelettes de mouton** san cotlet der mooton

You may also want:

A chicken	**Un poulet** an pooleh
A rabbit	**Un lapin** an lah-pan
A tongue	**Une langue** oon lahng

Other essential expressions [*see also p. 54*]:

Please can you . . .	**S'il vous plaît, pouvez-vous . . .** sil voo pleh, pooveh voo . . .
mince it?	**le hacher?** ler asheh
dice it?	**le découper en dés?** ler dehcoopeh ahn deh
trim the fat?	**enlever le gras?** ahnlerveh ler grah

Fish

ESSENTIAL INFORMATION

- The place to ask for:
  UNE POISSONNERIE (fish shop)
- Another key word to look for is **FRUITS DE MER** (seafood).
- Markets and large supermarkets usually have a fresh fish stall.
- Weight guide: 8 oz/250g minimum per person, for one meal of fish bought on the bone
  i.e. $\frac{1}{2}$ kg/500 g   for 2 people
  1 kg   for 4 people
  $1\frac{1}{2}$ kg   for 6 people

WHAT TO SAY

Purchase large fish and small shellfish by weight:

$\frac{1}{2}$ kilo of ...	**Un demi-kilo de*** ...
	an der-me keelo der ...
1 kilo of ...	**Un kilo de*** ...
	an keelo der ...
$1\frac{1}{2}$ kilos of ...	**Un kilo et demi de*** ...
	an keelo eh der-me der ...
anchovies	**anchois**
	ahn-shwah
cod	**morue**
	moroo
eel	**anguille**
	ahn-gweel
mussels	**moules**
	mool
oysters	**huîtres**
	weet
prawns	**crevettes roses**
	crer-vet rose
red mullet	**rougets**
	roosheh

* Use **d'** in front of words beginning with a vowel.

1½ kilos of ...	**Un kilo et demi de ...**
	an keelo eh der-me der ...
sardines	**sardines**
	sardeen
shrimps	**crevettes grises**
	crer-vet greez
turbot	**turbot**
	toorbo
whiting	**merlans**
	mairlahn

Some large fish can be purchased by the slice:

One slice of ...	**Une tranche de ...**
	oon trahnsh der ...
Two slices of ...	**Deux tranches de ...**
	der trahnsh der ...
Six slices of ...	**Six tranches de ...**
	see trahnsh der ...
cod	**cabillaud**
	cahbee-yo
salmon	**saumon**
	somon
tuna (fresh)	**thon**
	ton

For some shellfish and 'frying pan' fish, specify the number you want:

A crab, please	**Un crabe, s'il vous plaît**
	an crab sil voo pleh
A herring	**Un hareng**
	an ah-rahn
A lobster	**Une langouste/Un homard**
	oon lahngoost/an omar
A mackerel	**Un maquereau**
	an mackro
A scallop	**Une coquille de Saint-Jacques**
	oon cokee der san shack
A sole	**Une sole**
	oon sol
A trout	**Une truite**
	oon trweet
A whiting	**Un merlan**
	an mairlahn

Other essential expressions [*see also p. 54*]:

Please can you ...	**S'il vous plaît, pouvez-vous ...**
	sil voo pleh pooveh voo ...
take the heads off?	**enlever les têtes?**
	ahnlerveh leh tet
clean them?	**les vider?**
	leh veedeh
fillet them?	**les découper en filets?**
	leh dehcoopeh ahn feeleh

Eating and drinking out

Ordering a drink

ESSENTIAL INFORMATION

- The places to ask for: [*see p. 18*]
  BAR
  CAFÉ
- The price list of drinks (**TARIF DES CONSOMMATIONS**)
  must, by law, be displayed outside or in the window.
- There is a waiter service in all cafés and bars, but you can drink
  at the bar or counter if you wish (cheaper).
- Always leave a tip of 10% or 15% of the bill unless you see
  SERVICE COMPRIS or **PRIX NETS** (service included) printed
  on the bill or on a notice.
- Bars and cafés serve both alcoholic and non-alcoholic drinks.
  There are no licensing laws and children are allowed in.

WHAT TO SAY

I'd like . . . please	**Je voudrais . . . s'il vous plaît**
	sher voodreh . . . sil voo pleh
a black coffee	**un café nature/un café noir**
	an cahfeh nahtoor/an cahfeh nwah
a coffee with cream	**un café crème**
	an cahfeh crem
a hot chocolate	**un chocolat chaud**
	an shocolah sho
a tea	**un thé**
	an teh
with milk	**au lait**
	o leh
with lemon	**au citron**
	o seetron
a Coca-Cola	**un Coca-Cola**
	an coca-cola
a glass of milk	**un verre de lait**
	an vair der leh

a lemonade	**une limonade**
	oon leemonad
a lemon squash	**une citronnade**
	oon seetronad
a mineral water	**un Perrier**
	an pair-yeh
an orangeade	**une orangeade**
	oon orahn-shad
an orange juice	**un jus d'orange**
	an shoo dorahnsh
a grape juice	**un jus de raisin**
	an shoo der rehzan
a pineapple juice	**un jus d'ananas**
	an shoo dahnahnah
a beer	**une bière**
	oon be-air
a draught beer	**une bière pression**
	óon be-air pressee-on
a light ale	**une Kanterbrau**
	oon Kanterbro
a lager	**une Pils**
	oon pils
a half	**un demi**
	an der-me
A glass of ...	**Un verre de ...**
	an vair der ...
Two glasses of ...	**Deux verres de ...**
	der vair der ...
red wine	**vin rouge**
	van roosh
white wine	**vin blanc**
	van blahn
rosé wine	**vin rosé**
	van roseh
dry	**sec**
	sek
sweet	**doux**
	doo
sparkling wine	**vin mousseux**
	van moosser
champagne	**champagne**
	shampan

A whisky	**Un whisky**
	an whisky
with ice	**avec des glaçons**
	ahvec deh glasson
with water	**à l'eau**
	ah lo
with soda	**avec soda**
	ahvec soda
A gin	**Un gin**
	an gin
and tonic	**avec Schweppes**
	ahvec shwep
with lemon	**avec citron**
	ahvec seetron
A brandy/cognac	**Un cognac**
	an cognac

These are local drinks you may like to try:

un Calvados	apple brandy
an calvados	
un citron pressé	freshly squeezed lemon drink
an seetron presseh	
un cointreau	orange liqueur (digestive)
an cwentro	
un diabolo-menthe	lemonade and mint cordial
an dee-ahbolo-mahnt	
une eau de vie	a type of brandy (digestive)
oon o der vee	
une infusion	herb tea (drunk after meals)
oon anfoozee-on	
un muscat	a sweet red wine (apéritif)
an moo-skah	
un Cazanis/un Ricard/un Pernod/un pastis	drink made from aniseed and brandy (apéritif)
an cazanis/an reecar/an pairno/ an pass-teess	

Other essential expressions:

Miss! [*this does not sound abrupt in French*]	**Mademoiselle!**
	mad-mwahzel
Waiter!	**Garçon!**
	gar-son
The bill, please!	**L'addition, s'il vous plaît!**
	laddisee-on sil voo pleh
How much does that come to?	**Ça fait combien?**
	sah feh combee-an
Is service included?	**Est-ce que le service est compris?**
	esk ler sairvees eh compree
Where is the toilet, please?	**Où sont les WC, s'il vous plaît?**
	oo son leh veh-seh sil voo pleh

Ordering a snack

ESSENTIAL INFORMATION

- Look for a café or bar with these signs: **CASSE-CROÛTE À TOUTE HEURE** (snacks at any time) and **SANDWICHS**
- Look for the names of snacks (listed below) on signs in the window or on the pavement.
- In some regions mobile vans sell hot snacks. ● For cakes, see p. 61
- For ice-cream, see p. 63. ● For picnic-type snacks, see p. 68.

WHAT TO SAY

I'd like . . . please	**Je voudrais . . . s'il vous plaît** sher voodreh . . . sil voo pleh
a cheese sandwich	**un sandwich au fromage** an sandwich o fromash
a ham sandwich	**un sandwich au jambon** an sandwich o shahmbon
a pancake	**une crêpe** oon crep

These are some other snacks you may like to try:

une choucroûte garnie oon shoo-croot gahrnee	sauerkraut usually served with ham smoked bacon and sausage
un croque-monsieur an crok-mer-see-er	toasted ham and cheese sandwich
des frites deh freet	chips
un hot-dog an ot-dog	a hot dog
un sandwich au saucisson an sandwich o so-see-son	a salami sandwich
un sandwich au pâté an sandwich o pah-teh	a pâté sandwich

Some snacks e.g. chips may be sold at a variety of prices. You should add to the order:

5/10 francs worth of chips	**Cinq/dix francs de frites** sank/dee frahn der freet

[For other essential expressions, see 'Ordering a drink', p. 80.]

In a restaurant

ESSENTIAL INFORMATION

- The place to ask for: **UN RESTAURANT** [see p. 18.]
- You can eat at these places:
  RESTAURANT
  CAFÉ
  BUFFET (at stations)
  ROUTIERS (transport cafés)
  BRASSERIE (limited choice here)
  RELAIS
  AUBERGE
  RÔTISSERIE
  DRUGSTORE
  BISTRO
  LIBRE-SERVICE (self-service cafeterias on the
  outskirts of towns or in hypermarkets)
- By law, the menus must be displayed outside or in the window –
  and that is the *only* way to judge if a place is right for your needs.
- Self-service restaurants are not unknown (see above), but all other
  places have waiter service.
- Leave a tip unless you see **SERVICE COMPRIS** on the bill or on
  the menu.
- Children's portions are not usually available.
- Eating times: usually from 11.30–2, and from 7–10, but these vary
  a great deal according to the type of establishment.

WHAT TO SAY

May I book a table?	**Puis-je réserver une table?** pweesh reh-zairveh oon tab
I've booked a table	**J'ai réservé une table** sheh reh-zairveh oon tab
A table ...	**Une table ...** oon tab ...
for one	**pour une personne** poor oon pair-son
for three	**pour trois personnes** poor trwah pair-son
The à la carte menu, please	**La carte, s'il vous plaît** la cart sil voo pleh

The fixed price menu	**Le menu à prix fixe**
	ler mer-noo ah pree fix
The 25 franc menu	**Le menu à vingt-cinq francs**
	ler mer-noo ah vant-san frahn
The tourist menu	**Le menu touristique**
	ler mer-noo touristeek
Today's special menu	**Le menu du jour**
	ler mer-noo doo shoor
The wine list	**La carte des vins**
	lah cart deh van
What's this, please? [*point to menu*]	**Qu'est ce que c'est ça, s'il vous plaît**
	kesk seh sah sil voo pleh
A carafe of wine, please	**Une carafe de vin, s'il vous plaît**
	oon car-af der van sil voo pleh
A quarter (25 cc)	**Un quart**
	an car
A half (50 cc)	**Une demi-carafe**
	oon der-me car-af
A glass	**Un verre**
	an vair
A bottle/a litre	**Une bouteille/un litre**
	oon bootay/an leet
A half-bottle	**Une demi-bouteille**
	oon der-me bootay
Red/white/rosé/house wine	**Du vin rouge/blanc/rosé/maison**
	doo van roosh/blahn/roseh/mehzo
Some more bread, please	**Encore du pain, s'il vous plaît**
	ahncor doo pan sil voo pleh
Some more wine	**Encore du vin**
	ahncor doo van
Some oil	**De l'huile**
	der lweel
Some vinegar	**Du vinaigre**
	doo veeneg
Some salt	**Du sel**
	doo sel
Some pepper	**Du poivre**
	doo pwahv
Some water	**De l'eau**
	der lo
With/without (garlic)	**Sans/avec de (l'ail)**
	sahn/ahvec der (lie)

How much does that come to?	**Ça fait combien?**
	sah feh combee-an
Is service included?	**Est-ce que le service est compris?**
	esk ler sairvees eh compree
Where is the toilet, please?	**Où sont les WC s'il vous plaît?**
	oon son leh veh-seh sil voo pleh
Miss! [*this does not sound abrupt in French*]	**Mademoiselle!**
	mad-mwahzel
Waiter!	**Garçon!**
	gar-son
The bill, please	**L'addition, s'il vous plaît**
	laddisee-on sil voo pleh

Key words for courses, as seen on some menus: [*Only ask this question if you want the waiter to remind you of the choice.*]

What have you got in the way of . . .	**Qu'est-ce que vous avez comme . . .**
	kesk voozahveh com
starters?	**hors d'œuvre?**
	or derv
soup?	**soupe?**
	soup
egg dishes?	**œufs?**
	er
fish?	**poisson?**
	pwah-son
meat?	**viande?**
	vee-ahnd
game?	**gibier?**
	sheeb-yeh
fowl?	**volaille?**
	vol-eye
vegetables?	**légumes?**
	lehgoom
cheese?	**fromages?**
	fromash
fruit?	**fruits?**
	frwee
ice-cream?	**glaces?**
	glass
dessert?	**dessert?**
	deh-sair

UNDERSTANDING THE MENU

- You will find the names of the principal ingredients of most dishes on these pages:

Starters p. 68	Fruit p. 71
Meat p. 74	Cheese p. 70
Fish p. 77	Ice-cream p. 63
Vegetables p. 72	Dessert p. 61

Used together with the following lists of cooking and menu terms they should help you to decode the menu.
- These cooking and menu terms are for understanding only – not for speaking.

Cooking and menu terms

à l'anglaise	boiled
au beurre	with butter
au beurre noir	fried in sizzling butter
bien cuit	well done
bisque	shellfish soup
blanquette	cooked in a creamy sauce
au bleu	boiled in water, oil and thyme (fish) very rare (meat)
bonne femme	baked with wine and vegetables
bouilli	boiled
braisé	braised
en broche	spit-roasted
en cocotte	stewed
coquilles	cooked in a white sauce and browned under the grill
en croûte	in a pastry case
en daube	braised in a wine stock
à l'étouffée	stewed
farci	stuffed
au four	baked
à la française	cooked with lettuce and onion
frit	fried
froid	cold
fumé	smoked
garni	served with vegetables or chips
au gratin	sprinkled with breadcrumbs and browned under the grill

grillé	grilled
haché	minced
maître d'hôtel	served with butter mixed with parsley and lemon juice
Marengo	cooked in oil, tomatoes and white wine
mousseline	mousse
Parmentier	containing potatoes
poché	poached
à point	medium
à la provençale	cooked with garlic, tomatoes, olive oil, olives, onions and herbs
rôti	roasted
saignant	rare
salade	served with oil and vinegar dressing
sauce béarnaise'	vinegar, egg yolks, white wine, butter, shallots and tarragon
sauce béchamel	flour, butter and milk
sauce bourguignonne	red wine sauce with herbs, onions and spices
sauce madère	cooked in Madeira wine
sauce Mornay	cheese sauce
sauce piquante	sharp vinegar sauce with chopped gherkins and herbs
sauté	fried slowly in butter
en terrine	preparation of meat, game or fowl baked in a terrine (casserole) and served cold
à la vapeur	steamed
Vichy	garnished with carrots
vinaigrette	with oil and vinegar dressing

Further words to help you understand the menu

assiette anglaise	cold meat and salad
boudin	black pudding
bouillabaisse	rich fish soup in which a variety of fish and shell fish have been cooked. Soup and fish are served in separate dishes
champignons	mushrooms
chantilly	cream whipped with icing sugar

choucroûte	sauerkraut
compote	stewed fruit
consommé	clear broth
crudités	raw vegetables and salads served as starters
cuisses de grenouilles	frogs' legs
escalopes panées	veal escalopes fried in egg and breadcrumbs
escargots	snails
flan	egg custard
moules	mussels
potage	vegetable soup
quenelles	fish or meat fingers cooked in a white sauce
ragoût	stew
ratatouille	a vegetable stew
ris de veau	veal sweetbreads
sorbet	water ice
tournedos	fillet steak

Health

ESSENTIAL INFORMATION

- For details of reciprocal health agreements between the UK and France, ask for leaflet SA30 at your local Department of Health and Social Security a month before leaving, or ask your travel agent.
- In addition, it is preferable to purchase a medical insurance policy through the travel agent, a broker or a motoring organization.
- Take your own 'first line' first aid kit with you.
- For minor disorders and treatment at a chemist's, see p. 40.
- For finding your way to a doctor, dentist, chemist or Health and Social Security Office (for reimbursement), see p. 18.
- Once in France, decide a definite plan of action in case of serious illness: communicate your problem to a near neighbour, the receptionist or someone you see regularly. You are then dependent on that person helping you obtain treatment.
- To find a doctor in an emergency, look for:
Médecins (in the Yellow Pages of the telephone directory)
Les Urgences (casualty department)
H
Hôpital] (hospital)

What's the matter?

I have a pain . . .	**J'ai mal . . .**
	sheh mal . . .
in my abdomen	**au ventre**
	o vahnt
in my ankle	**à la cheville**
	ah lah sher-vee
in my arm	**au bras**
	o bra
in my back	**au dos**
	o doh
in my bladder	**à la vessie**
	ah lah vessee
in my bowels	**à l'intestin**
	ah lantestan

I have a pain . . .	J'ai mal . . .
	sheh mal . . .
in my breast	au sein
	o san
in my chest	à la poitrine
	ah lah pwahtreen
in my ear	à l'oreille
	ah loray
in my eye	à l'œil
	ah ler-yer
in my foot	au pied
	o pee-eh
in my head	à la tête
	ah lah tet
in my heel	au talon
	o tah-lon
in my jaw	à la mâchoire
	ah lah mah-shwah
in my kidney	au rein
	o ran
in my leg	à la jambe
	ah lah shahmb
in my lung	au poumon
	o poomon
in my neck	au cou
	o coo
in my penis	au pénis
	o penneess
in my shoulder	à l'épaule
	ah lehpol
in my stomach	à l'estomac
	ah lestomah
in my testicle	au testicule
	o testicool
in my throat	à la gorge
	ah lah gorsh
in my vagina	au vagin
	o vah-shan
in my wrist	au poignet
	o pwah-nee-eh
I have a pain here [*point*]	J'ai mal ici
	sheh mal ee-see

I have a toothache — **J'ai mal aux dents**
sheh mal o dahn

I have broken ... — **J'ai cassé ...**
sheh casseh ...

  my dentures — **mon dentier**
mon dahnt-yeh

  my glasses — **mes lunettes**
meh loonet

I have lost ... — **J'ai perdu ...**
sheh pairdoo ...

  my contact lenses — **mes verres de contact**
meh vair der contact

  a filling — **un plombage**
an plombash

My child is ill — **Mon enfant est malade**
mon ahnfahn eh mal-ad

He/she has a pain in his/her ... — **Il/elle a mal ...***
il/el ah mal ...

  ankle [see list above] — **à la cheville**
ah lah sher-vee

How bad is it?

I'm ill — **Je suis malade**
sher swee mal-ad

It's urgent — **C'est urgent**
set oorshahn

It's serious — **C'est grave**
seh grav

It's not serious — **Ce n'est pas grave**
ser neh pah grav

It hurts — **Ça me fait mal**
sah mer feh mal

It hurts a lot — **Ça me fait très mal**
sah mer feh treh mal

It doesn't hurt much — **Ça ne me fait pas très mal**
sah ner mer feh pah treh mal

The pain occurs ... — **La douleur revient ...**
lah dooler rer-vee-an ...

  every quarter of an hour — **tous les quarts d'heure**
too leh car der

* For boys use 'il', for girls use 'elle'.

The pain occurs ...	**La douleur revient ...**
	lah dooler rer-vee-an ...
every half hour	**toutes les demi-heures**
	toot leh der-me-er
every hour	**toutes les heures**
	toot leh zer
every day	**tous les jours**
	too leh shoor
It hurts most of the time	**C'est une douleur continue**
	set-oon dooler conteenoo
I've had it for ...	**Ça me fait mal depuis ...**
	sah mer feh mal der-pwee ...
one hour/one day	**une heure/un jour**
	ooner/an shoor
two hours/two days	**deux heures/deux jours**
	der-zer/der shoor
It's a ...	**C'est une ...**
	set oon ...
sharp pain	**douleur aiguë**
	dooler eggoo
dull ache	**douleur sourde**
	dooler soord
nagging pain	**douleur irritante**
	dooler irritahnt
I feel ...	**J'ai ...**
	sheh ...
dizzy	**des vertiges**
	deh vairteesh
sick	**la nausée**
	lah nozeh
I feel ...	**Je me sens ...**
	sher mer sahn ...
weak	**faible**
	feb
feverish	**fiévreux/fiévreuse***
	fee-evrer/fee-evrerz

Already under treatment for something else?

I take ... regularly [*show*]	**Je prends ... régulièrement**
	sher prahn ... rehgool-yair-mahn

* Men use the first alternative, women the second.

this medicine	**ce médicament**
	ser meh-deecah-mahn
these pills	**ces pilules**
	seh peelool
I have ...	**J'ai ...**
	sheh ...
a heart condition	**le cœur malade**
	ler ker mal-ad
haemorrhoids	**des hémorroïdes**
	deh zeh-moro-eed
rheumatism	**des rhumatismes**
	deh rheumateesm
I am ...	**Je suis ...**
	sher swee ...
diabetic	**diabétique**
	dee-ah-beh-teek
asthmatic	**asthmatique**
	asthmateek
pregnant	**enceinte**
	ahn-sant
allergic to (penicillin)	**allergique à (la pénicilline)**
	allersheek ah (lah penicillin)

Other essential expressions

Please can you help?	**Pouvez-vous m'aider s'il vous plaît?**
	pooveh-voo med-eh sil voo pleh
A doctor, please	**Un docteur, s'il vous plaît**
	an doc-ter sil voo pleh
A dentist	**Un dentiste**
	an dahnteest
I don't speak French	**Je ne parle pas français**
	sher ner parl pah frahn-seh
What time does ... arrive?	**A quelle heure arrive ...**
	ah keller ahreev ...
the doctor	**le docteur?**
	ler doc-ter
the dentist	**le dentiste?**
	ler dahntist

From the doctor: key sentences to understand

Take this . . .	**Prenez ceci . . .**
	prer-neh ser-see . . .
every day	**tous les jours**
	too leh shoor
every hour	**toutes les heures**
	toot leh zer
four times a day	**quatre fois par jour**
	kat fwah par shoor
Stay in bed	**Gardez le lit**
	gardeh ler lee
Don't travel . . .	**Ne voyagez pas . . .**
	ner vwah-yah-sheh pah . . .
for . . . days/weeks	**avant . . . jours/semaines**
	ahvahn . . . shoor/ser-men
You must go to hospital	**Vous devez aller à l'hôpital**
	voo der-veh ahleh ah lopetal

Problems: complaints, loss, theft

ESSENTIAL INFORMATION

- Problems with:
  camping facilities, see p. 34;
  household appliances, see p. 52;
  health, see p. 91;
  the car, see p. 106.
- If the worst comes to the worst, find the police station. To ask the way, see p. 18.
- Look for:
  GENDARMERIE (police)
  COMMISSARIAT DE POLICE (police station)
- If you lose your passport report the loss to the police and go to the nearest British Consulate.
- In an emergency, dial 17 for police/ambulance and 18 for the fire brigade.

COMPLAINTS

I bought this ...	**J'ai acheté ça ...**
	sheh ashteh sah ...
today	**aujourd'hui**
	o-shoordwee
yesterday	**hier**
	ee-air
on Monday [see p. 130]	**lundi**
	lerndee
It's no good (not suitable)	**Ça ne va pas**
	sah ner vah pah
It's no good (faulty)	**Il y a un défaut**
	il yah an dehfo
Look	**Regardez**
	rer-gardeh
Here [point]	**Ici**
	ee-see

Can you ...	Pouvez-vous ...
	pooveh-voo ...
change it?	l'échanger?
	leh-shahn-sheh
mend it?	le réparer?
	ler reh-pah-reh
give me a refund?	me rembourser?
	mer rahmboor-seh
Here's the receipt	Voici le reçu
	vwah-see ler rer-soo
Can I see the manager?	Puis-je voir le directeur?
	pweesh vwah ler deerecter

LOSS
[See also 'Theft' below: the lists are interchangeable]

I have lost ...	J'ai perdu ...
	sheh pairdoo ...
my bag	mon sac
	mon sac
my bracelet	mon bracelet
	mon brassleh
my camera	mon appareil photo
	mon appah-ray photo
my car keys	les clés de ma voiture
	leh cleh der mah vwahtoor
my car logbook	ma carte grise
	mah cart greez
my driving licence	mon permis de conduire
	mon pairmee der condweer
my insurance certificate	mon assurance
	mon assoorahns
my jewellery	mes bijoux
	meh bee-shoo
I have lost everything!	J'ai tout perdu!
	sheh too pairdoo

THEFT
[See also 'Loss' above: the lists are interchangeable.]

Someone has stolen ...	On m'a volé ...
	on mah voleh ...
my car	ma voiture
	mah vwahtoor

my car radio	**mon autoradio**
	mon autorah-dio
my keys	**mes clés**
	meh cleh
my money	**mon argent**
	mon arshahn
my necklace	**mon collier**
	mon col-yeh
my passport	**mon passeport**
	mon passpor
my radio	**mon transistor**
	mon transistor
my tickets	**mes billets**
	meh bee-yeh
my travellers' cheques	**mes traveller chèques**
	meh traveller shek
my wallet	**mon portefeuille**
	mon port-fey
my watch	**ma montre**
	mah mont
my luggage	**mes bagages**
	meh baggash

LIKELY REACTIONS: key words to understand

Wait	**Attendez**
	attahndeh
When?	**Quand?**
	kahn
Where?	**Où?**
	oo
Name?	**Nom?**
	nom
Address?	**Adresse?**
	address
I can't help you	**Je ne puis rien pour vous**
	sher ner pwee ree-an poor voo
Nothing to do with me	**Ce n'est pas ici qu'il faut s'adresser**
	ser neh pah ee-see kil fo saddresseh

The post office

ESSENTIAL INFORMATION

- To find a post office, see p. 18.
- Key words to look for:
  POSTES
  POSTE, TÉLÉGRAPHE, TÉLÉPHONE (PTT)
  POSTES ET TÉLÉCOMMUNICATIONS (PT)
- Look for this sign:

- It is best to buy stamps at the tobacconist's. Only go to the post office for more complicated transactions, like telegrams.
- Look for these signs on the shop.
- Letter boxes are yellow (red in Belgium).
- For poste restante you should show your passport at the counter marked **POSTE RESTANTE** in the main post office, and pay a small charge.

WHAT TO SAY

To England, please	**Pour l'Angleterre, s'il vous plaît** poor lahng-tair sil voo pleh

[*Hand letters, cards or parcels over the counter.*]

To Australia	**Pour l'Australie** poor lostrah-lee
To the United States	**Pour les États-Unis** poor leh zehtah-zoonee

[*For other countries, see p. 134.*]

How much is ...	**C'est combien ...** seh combee-an ...
this parcel (to Canada)?	**ce colis (pour le Canada)?** ser collee (poor ler canada)
a letter (to Australia)?	**une lettre (pour l'Australie)?** oon let (poor lostrah-lee)
a postcard (to England)?	**une carte postale (pour l'Angleterre)?** oon cart postahl (poor lahng-tair)
Air mail	**Par avion** par ahvee-on
Surface mail	**Ordinaire** ordeenair
One stamp, please	**Un timbre, s'il vous plaît** an tamb sil voo pleh
Two stamps	**Deux timbres** der tamb
One (1F 50) stamp	**Un timbre à (un franc cinquante)** an tamb ah (an frahn sankahnt)
I'd like to send a telegram	**Je voudrais envoyer un télégramme** sher voodreh ahn-vwah-yeh an telegram

Telephoning

ESSENTIAL INFORMATION

- Unless you read and speak French well, it's best not to make phone calls by yourself. Go to the main post office and write the town and number you want on a piece of paper. Add **avec préavis** if you want a person-to-person call or **PCV** if you want to reverse the charges.
- Public phones are located in perspex kiosks.
- To ask the way to a public phone, see p. 18.
- To make a call from an automatic public phone:
  put the appropriate coins in the slot. Lift the receiver. Wait for dialling tone. Dial. Put in more money when the sign **Épuisé** lights up.
- To call the operator, dial 10, but you have to pay!
- To make a call from a café you will have to buy a **jeton** (sold in cafés and post offices) to use instead of a coin. As above, insert the **jeton** and wait for a dialling tone.
- For international calls dial 19. Wait for second buzzing noise and then dial 44 for Great Britain (and London) or 1 for the United States. Then dial the town/area code number and the subscriber's number.

WHAT TO SAY

Where can I make a telephone call?	**Où puis-je téléphoner?** oo pweesh telephoneh
Local/abroad	**Dans la région/à l'étranger** dahn lah resh-yon/ah lettrahn-sheh
I'd like this number . . . [*show number*]	**Je voudrais ce numéro . . .** sher voodreh ser noomehro . . .
in England	**en Angleterre** ahn ahng-tair
in Canada	**au Canada** o canada
in the USA	**aux États-Unis** o zehtah- zoonee

[*For other countries, see p. 134.*]

Can you dial it for me, please?	**Pouvez-vous me l'appeler, s'il vous plaît?**
	pooveh-voo mer lap-leh sil voo pleh
How much is it?	**C'est combien?**
	seh combee-an
Hello!	**Allô!**
	allo
May I speak to ... ?	**Puis-je parler à ... ?**
	pweesh parleh ah ...
Extension ...	**Poste ...**
	post ...
I'm sorry, I don't speak French	**Je regrette, je ne parle pas français**
	sher rer-gret sher ner parl pah frahn-seh
Do you speak English?	**Parlez-vous anglais?**
	parleh-voo ahngleh
Thank you. I'll phone back	**Merci. Je rappellerai**
	mair-see sher rappel-reh
Goodbye	**Au revoir**
	o rer-vwah

LIKELY REACTIONS

That's 4 francs 50	**Ça fait quatre francs cinquante**
	sah feh kat frahn sankahnt
Cabin number (3)	**Cabine numéro (trois)**
	cabin noomehro (trwah)

[For numbers, see p. 126.]

Don't hang up	**Ne quittez pas**
	ner keeteh pah
I'm trying to connect you	**J'essaie de vous passer l'abonné**
	shesseh de voo pah-seh lahboneh
You're through	**Parlez**
	parleh
There's a delay	**Il y a une attente**
	il yah oon attahnt
I'll try again	**J'essaie encore (une fois)**
	shesseh ahncor (oon fwah)

Changing cheques and money

ESSENTIAL INFORMATION

- Finding your way to a bank or change bureau, see p. 18.
- Look for these words on buildings:
  BANQUE
  CRÉDIT
  SOCIÉTÉ GÉNÉRALE
  BUREAU DE CHANGE
  CHANGE
- To cash your normal cheques, exactly as at home, use your banker's card where you see the Eurocheque sign. Write in English, in pounds.
- Exchange rate information might show the pound as:
  £, L, Livre Sterling, L St, or even GB.
- Have your passport handy.

WHAT TO SAY

I'd like to cash ...	**Je voudrais encaisser ...**
	sher voodreh ahn-kesseh ...
this travellers' cheque	**ce traveller chèque**
	ser traveller shek
these travellers' cheques	**ces traveller chèques**
	seh traveller shek
this cheque	**ce chèque**
	ser shek
I'd like to change this into French francs	**Je voudrais changer ceci en francs français**
	sher voodreh shan-sheh ser-see ahn frahn frahn-seh
Here's ...	**Voici ...**
	vwah-see ...
my banker's card	**ma carte**
	mah cart
my passport	**mon passeport**
	mon passpor

For excursions into neighbouring countries

I'd like to change this . . .	**Je voudrais changer ceci . . .**
[*show bank notes*]	sher voodreh shahn-sheh ser-see . . .
into Austrian schillings	**en schillings autrichiens**
	ahn shilling otreesh-yan
into Belgian francs	**en francs belges**
	ahn frahn belsh
into German marks	**en marks**
	ahn mark
into Italian lira	**en lires**
	ahn leer
into Spanish pesetas	**en pesetas**
	ahn pesetas
into Swiss francs	**en francs suisses**
	ahn frahn sweess
What's the rate of exchange?	**Quel est le taux de change?**
	kelleh ler to der shahnsh

LIKELY REACTIONS

Passport, please	**Passeport, s'il vous plaît**
	passpor sil voo pleh
Sign here	**Signez ici**
	seen-yeh ee-see
Your banker's card, please	**Votre carte, s'il vous plaît**
	vot cart sil voo pleh
Go to the cash desk	**Passez à la caisse**
	passeh ah lah kess

Car travel

ESSENTIAL INFORMATION

- Finding a filling station or garage, see p. 18.
- Is it a self-service station? Look out for **LIBRE SERVICE o SERVEZ-VOUS.**
- Grades of petrol:
  NORMALE
  ORDINAIRE] (2 star, standard)
  SUPER (CARBURANT) (3 star and above, premium)
  GAS-OIL (diesel)
- 1 gallon is about 4½ litres (accurate enough up to 6 gallons).
- For car repairs, look for:
  DÉPANNAGE (repairs)
  GARAGE (garage)
  MÉCANICIEN (mechanic)
  CARROSSERIE (for body work)
- Petrol stations outside towns will sometimes close from 12–3.
- In the case of a breakdown or an emergency look for the TC (French Touring Club) sign, or dial 6969 (**Touring Secours**) from any telephone box.
- Unfamiliar road signs and warnings, see p. 121.

WHAT TO SAY

[*For numbers, see p. 126.*]

(Nine) litres	(Neuf) litres
	(nerf) leet
(Two hundred) francs	(Deux cents) francs
	(der sahn) frahn
of standard	d'ordinaire
	dordeenair
of premium	de super
	der soopair
of diesel	de gas-oil
	der gazwahl
Fill it up, please	Faites le plein, s'il vous plaît
	fet ler plan sil voo pleh

Can you check . . .
Pouvez-vous vérifier . . .
pooveh voo vehrif-yeh . . .

the oil?
l'huile?
lweel

the battery?
la batterie?
lah battree

the radiator?
le radiateur?
ler raddee-atter

the tyres?
les pneus?
leh pner

I've run out of petrol
Je suis en panne d'essence
sher swee ahn pan dessahns

Can I borrow a can, please?
Puis-je emprunter un bidon s'il vous plaît?
pweesh ahmprernteh an beedon sil voo pleh

My car has broken down
Ma voiture est en panne
mah vwahtoor eh ahn pan

My car won't start
Ma voiture ne démarre pas
mah vwahtoor ner deh-mar pah

I've had an accident
J'ai eu un accident
sheh oo an accidahn

I've lost my car keys
J'ai perdu les clés de ma voiture
sheh pairdoo leh cleh der mah vwahtoor

My car is . . .
Ma voiture est . . .
mah vwahtoor eh . . .

two kilometres away
à deux kilomètres
ah der keelomet

three kilometres away
à trois kilomètres
ah trwah keelomet

Can you help me, please?
Pouvez-vous m'aider, s'il vous plaît?
pooveh voo med-eh sil voo pleh

Do you do repairs?
Est-ce que vous faites les réparations?
esk voo fet leh rehpahrah-see-on

I have a puncture
J'ai une crevaison
sheh oon crer-veh-zon

I have a broken windscreen
Mon pare-brise est cassé
mon par-breez eh casseh

I think the problem is here . . . [point]
Je crois que c'est ça qui ne va pas . . .
sher crwah ker seh sah kee ner vah pah . . .

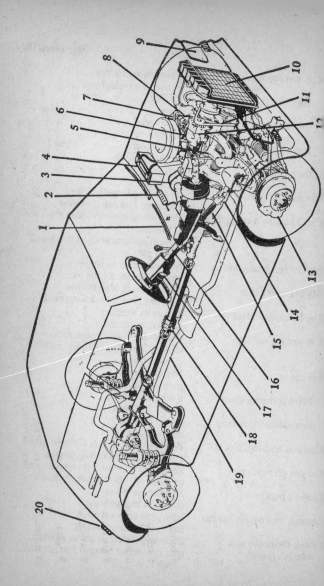

1 windscreen wipers	essuie-glace		11 fan belt	courroie de ventilation
	eswee-glass			coorwah der vahnteelah-see-on
2 fuses	fusibles		12 generator	génerateur
	foozeeb			shehneh-ratter
3 heater	chauffage		13 brakes	freins
	shofash			fran
4 battery	batterie		14 clutch	embrayage
	battree			ahmbreh-yash
5 engine	moteur		15 gear box	boîte à vitesses
	motor			bwaht ah veetess
6 fuel pump	pompe à essence		16 steering	direction
	pomp ah essahns			deerec-see-on
7 starter motor	démarreur		17 ignition	allumage
	dehmah-rer			alloomash
8 carburettor	carburateur		18 transmission	transmission
	carbooratter			trahnsme-see-on
9 lights	phares		19 exhaust	tuyau d'échappement
	far			twee-yo dehshap-mahn
10 radiator	radiateur		20 indicators	clignotants
	raddee-atter			cleen-yotahn

I don't know what's wrong	**Je ne sais pas ce qui ne va pas**
	sher ner say pah ser kee ner vah pah
Can you ...	**Pouvez-vous ...**
	pooveh-voo ...
repair the fault?	**faire la réparation?**
	fair lah reh-pahrah-see-on
come and look?	**venir voir?**
	ver-neer vwah
estimate the cost?	**me donner un prix?**
	mer donneh an pree
write it down?	**l'écrire?**
	lehcreer
Do you accept these coupons?	**Acceptez-vous ces coupons?**
	accepteh-voo seh coopon
How long will the repair take?	**Combien de temps prendra la réparation?**
	combee-an der tahn prahndrah lah rehpahrah-see-on
When will the car be ready?	**La voiture sera prête quand?**
	lah vwahtoor ser-rah pret kahn
Can I see the bill?	**Puis-je voir la note?**
	pweesh vwah lah not
This is my insurance document	**Voici mon assurance**
	vwah-see mon assoorahns

HIRING A CAR

Can I hire a car?	**Puis-je louer une voiture?**
	pweesh loo-eh oon vwahtoor
I need a car ...	**J'ai besoin d'une voiture ...**
	sheh ber-zwan doon vwahtoor ...
for two people	**pour deux personnes**
	poor der pair-son
for five people	**pour cinq personnes**
	poor san pair-son
for one day	**pour une journée**
	poor oon shoorneh
for five days	**pour cinq jours**
	poor san shoor
for a week	**pour une semaine**
	poor oon ser-men

Can you write down . . .

Pouvez-vous écrire . . .
pooveh-voo ehcreer . . .

the deposit to pay?

les arrhes à verser?
leh zar ah vair-seh

the charge per kilometre?

le tarif au kilomètre?
ler tariff o keelomet

the daily charge?

le tarif à la journée?
ler tariff ah lah shoorneh

the cost of insurance?

le montant de l'assurance?
ler montahn der lassoorahns

Can I leave it in (Paris)?

Puis-je la laisser à (Paris)?
pweesh lah lesseh ah (pahree)

What documents do I need?

Quels papiers me faut-il?
kel pap-yeh mer fo-til

LIKELY REACTIONS

I don't do repairs

Je ne fais pas les réparations
sher ner feh-pah leh rehpahrahsee-on

Where's your car?

Où est votre voiture?
oo eh vot vwahtoor

What make is it?

C'est quelle marque?
seh kel mark

Come back tomorrow/on
Monday

Revenez demain/lundi
rer-venneh der-man/lerndee

[*For days of the week, see p. 130.*]

We don't hire cars

On ne fait pas la location
on ner feh pah lah locah-see-on

Your driving licence, please

Votre permis, s'il vous plaît
vot pairmee sil voo pleh

The mileage is unlimited

Le kilométrage n'est pas limité
ler keelomeh-trash neh pah limiteh

Public transport

ESSENTIAL INFORMATION

- Finding the way to the bus station, bus stop, tram stop, railway station and taxi rank, see p. 18.
- Remember that queuing for buses is unheard of!
- Taxis can be found at taxi ranks in the main areas of a town, especially at the railway station.
- These are the different types of trains, graded according to speed (slowest to fastest):
  AUTORAIL
  EXPRESS
  RAPIDE (a supplement is sometimes payable
  if the train is an exceptionally fast one)
  CORAIL (rolling stock: air-conditioned inter-city luxury train)
  TRANS EUROP EXPRESS (TEE) (first class only,
  supplement payable on these trains)
- Key words on signs [see also p. 121]:
  ACCÈS AUX QUAIS (to the trains)
  ARRÊT D'AUTOBUS (bus stop)
  BILLETS (tickets, ticket office)
  CONSIGNE (left luggage)
  ENTRÉE (entrance)
  HORAIRE (timetable)
  INTERDIT(E) (forbidden)
  LOCATIONS (bookings)
  MONTÉE (entrance for buses)
  N'OUBLIEZ PAS DE COMPOSTER (don't forget to validate)
  RENSEIGNEMENTS (information)
  QUAI (platform)
  SORTIE (exit)
  VOIE (platform)
- As French Railways have abolished ticket control at platform barriers, *you* must validate your ticket by using one of the orange coloured date stamping machines provided at platform entrances *before* departure. If you fail to do so, you will be liable to a fine of up to 20% of your fare. Keep an eye out for the sign shown on the opposite page.

Accès aux quais Au-delà
de cette limite
votre billet
doit être valide
compostez-le

However, these regulations do not apply to international tickets
purchased outside France.
● There is a flat rate for underground tickets and it is cheaper to
buy a **carnet** (a book of ten tickets). In Paris, bus and underground tickets are interchangeable.
● Children under 10 pay half-fare on trains but if you buy the ticket
in this country, children under 12 can travel half-fare.

WHAT TO SAY

Where does the train for (Paris) **De quelle voie part le train de (Paris)?**
leave from?
  der kel vwah par ler tran der (pahree)

At what time does the train **A quelle heure part le train de**
leave for (Paris)? **(Paris)?**
  a keller par ler tran der (pahree)

At what time does the train **A quelle heure le train arrive-t-il à**
arrive in (Paris) **(Paris)?**
  ah keller ler tran ahreev-til ah
  (pahree)

Is this the train for (Paris)? **Est-ce le train de (Paris)?**
  ess ler tran der (pahree)

Where does the bus for **D'où part l'autobus de (Toulouse)?**
(Toulouse) leave from? doo par lotoboos der (too-looz)

At what time does the bus **A quelle heure part l'autobus de**
leave for (Toulouse)? **(Toulouse)?**
  ah keller par lotoboos der (too-looz)

At what time does the bus **A quelle heure l'autobus arrive-t-il à**
arrive in (Toulouse)? **(Toulouse)?**
  ah keller lotoboos ahreev-til ah
  (too-looz)

Is this the bus for (Toulouse)? **Est-ce l'autobus de (Toulouse)?**
  ess lotoboos der (too-looz)

Do I have to change? **Faut-il changer?**
  fo-til shahn-sheh

Where does . . . leave from?	D'où part . . .?
	doo par
the bus	l'autobus
	lotoboos
the train	le train
	ler tran
the underground	le métro
	ler metro
the boat/ferry	le bateau/le ferry
	ler bahto/ler ferry
for the airport	pour l'aéroport
	poor lah-ehropor
for the beach	pour la plage
	poor lah plash
for the cathedral	pour la cathédrale
	poor lah cattedrahl
for the market place	pour la place du marché
	poor lah plass doo marsheh
for the railway station	pour la gare
	poor lah gar
for St John's Church	pour l'église St Jean
	poor leh-gleez san-shahn
for the swimming pool	pour la piscine
	poor lah pee-seen
for the town centre	pour le centre de la ville
	poor ler sahnt der lah veel
for the town hall	pour la mairie
	poor lah meh-ree
Is this . . .	Est-ce . . .
	ess . . .
the bus for the market place?	l'autobus pour la place du marché?
	lotoboos poor lah plass doo marsheh
the tram for the railway station?	le tram pour la gare?
	ler tram poor lah gar
Where can I get a taxi?	Où puis-je trouver un taxi?
	oo pweesh trooveh an taxee
Can you put me off at the right stop, please?	Pouvez-vous me dire où je dois descendre?
	pooveh-voo mer deer oo sher dwah dessahnd
Can I book a seat?	Puis-je réserver une place?
	pweesh reh-zairveh oon plass

A single	**Un aller**
	an alleh
A return	**Un aller-retour**
	an alleh rer-toor
First class	**Première classe**
	prem-yair class
Second class	**Deuxième classe**
	der-zee-em class
One adult	**Un adulte**
	an ahdoolt
Two adults	**Deux adultes**
	der zahdoolt
and one child	**et un enfant**
	eh an ahnfahn
and two children	**et deux enfants**
	eh der zahnfahn
How much is it?	**C'est combien?**
	seh combee-an

LIKELY REACTIONS

Over there	**Là-bas**
	lah-bah
Here	**Ici**
	ee-see
Platform (1)	**Quai numéro (un)/(Première) voie**
	keh noomehro (an)/(prem-yair)
	vwah
At (4 o'clock)	**A (quatre heures)**
[For times, see p. 128.]	ah (kat er)
Change at (Vichy)	**Changez à (Vichy)**
	shahn-sheh ah (vee-she)
Change at (the town hall)	**Changez à (la mairie)**
	shahn-sheh ah (lah mairee)
This is your stop	**Voici votre arrêt**
	vwah-see vot ah-reh
There's only first class	**Il n'y a que des premières (classes)**
	il nee yah ker deh prem-yair (class)
There's a supplement	**Il y a un supplément**
	il yah an soopplehmahn

Leisure

ESSENTIAL INFORMATION

- Finding the way to a place of entertainment, see p. 18.
- For times of day, see p. 128.
- Important signs, see p. 121.
- In the more popular seaside resorts you have to pay to go on the beach and to hire deckchairs and sunshades.
- Smoking is forbidden in cinemas and theatres, unless otherwise specified.
- You should tip theatre usherettes.

WHAT TO SAY

At what time does . . . open?	A quelle heure ouvre . . . ? ah keller oov . . .
the art gallery	le musée d'art ler moozeh dar
the botanical garden	le jardin botanique ler shardan botaneek
the cinema	le cinéma ler cinema
the concert hall	la salle de concerts lah sal der con-sair
the disco	la discothèque la discotek
the museum	le musée ler moozeh
the night club	la boîte de nuit lah bwaht der nwee
the sports stadium	le stade ler stad
the swimming pool	la piscine lah pee-seen
the theatre	le théâtre ler teh-art
the zoo	le zoo ler zo-o

At what time does . . . close?	**A quelle heure ferme . . . ?**
	ah keller fairm . . .
the art gallery	**le musée d'art**
[see above list]	ler moozeh dar
At what time does . . . start?	**A quelle heure commence . . . ?**
	ah keller commahns . . .
the cabaret	**le cabaret**
	ler cabaret
the concert	**le concert**
	ler con-sair
the film	**le film**
	ler film
the match	**le match**
	ler match
the play	**la pièce**
	lah pee-ess
the race	**la course**
	lah coorss
How much is it . . .	**C'est combien . . .**
	seh combee-an . . .
for an adult?	**pour un adulte?**
	poor an ahdoolt
for a child?	**pour un enfant?**
	poor an ahnfahn
Two adults, please	**Deux adultes, s'il vous plaît**
	der zahdoolt sil voo pleh
Three children, please	**Trois enfants, s'il vous plaît**
	trwah zahnfahn sil voo pleh
[state price, if there is a choice]	
Stalls/circle/sun/shade	**Orchestre/balcon/au soleil/à l'ombre**
	orkest/balcon/o solay/ah lomb
Do you have . . .	**Avez-vous . . .**
	ahveh-voo . . .
a programme?	**un programme?**
	an program
a guide book?	**un guide?**
	an gheed
Where is the toilet, please?	**Où sont les WC, s'il vous plaît?**
	oo son leh veh-seh sil voo pleh
Where's the cloakroom?	**Où est le vestiaire?**
	oo eh ler vestee-air

I would like lessons in . . .	Je voudrais des leçons de . . .
	sher voodreh deh ler-son der . . .
sailing	voile
	vwahl
skiing	ski
	skee
sub-aqua diving	plongée sous-marine
	plonsheh soo-marine
water skiing	ski nautique
	skee noteek
Can I hire . . .	Puis-je louer . . .
	pweesh loo-eh . . .
some skis?	des skis?
	deh skee
some skiboots?	des chaussures de ski?
	deh shossooer der skee
a boat?	un bateau?
	an bahto
a fishing rod?	une canne à pêche?
	oon can ah pesh
a deckchair?	une chaise-longue?
	oon shez-long
a sun umbrella?	un parasol?
	an parasol
the necessary equipment?	le nécessaire?
	ler nesseh-sair
How much is it . . .	C'est combien . . .
	seh combee-an . . .
per day/per hour?	par jour/de l'heure?
	par shoor/der ler
Must I have a licence?	Faut-il un permis?
	fo-til an pairmee

Asking if things are allowed

ESSENTIAL INFORMATION

● May one smoke here?
  May we smoke here?
  May I smoke here?
  Can one smoke here?
  Can we smoke here?
  Can I smoke here?

On peut fumer ici?

● All these English variations can be expressed in one way in French.
  To save space, only the first English version (May one . . . ?) is
  shown below.

WHAT TO SAY

Excuse me, please	**Excusez-moi**
	excooseh mwah
May one . . .	**On peut . . .**
	on per . . .
camp here?	**camper ici?**
	campeh ee-see
come in?	**entrer?**
	ahntreh
dance here?	**danser ici?**
	dahn seh ee-see
fish here?	**pêcher ici?**
	peh-sheh ee-see
get a drink here?	**avoir des boissons ici?**
	ahvwah deh bwah-son ee-see
get out this way?	**sortir par ici?**
	sorteer par ee-see
get something to eat here?	**manger quelque chose ici?**
	mahnsheh kelker shoz ee-see
leave one's things here?	**laisser ses affaires ici?**
	lesseh seh-zaffair ee-see
look around?	**regarder?**
	rer-gardeh
park here?	**se garer ici?**
	ser gahreh ee-see

May one ...	**On peut ...**
	on per ...
picnic here?	**pique-niquer ici?**
	peek-neekeh ee-see
sit here?	**s'asseoir ici?**
	sasswah ee-see
smoke here?	**fumer ici?**
	foomeh ee-see
swim here?	**nager ici?**
	nasheh ee-see
take photos here?	**prendre des photos ici?**
	prahnd deh photo ee-see
telephone here?	**téléphoner ici?**
	telephoneh ee-see
wait here?	**attendre ici?**
	attahnd ee-see

LIKELY REACTIONS

Yes, certainly	**Certainement**
	sairten-mahn
Help yourself	**Allez-y**
	alleh-zee
I think so	**Je crois**
	sher crwah
Or course	**Bien sûr**
	bee-an soor
Yes, but be careful	**Oui, mais faites attention**
	wee meh fet attahn-see-on
No, certainly not	**Certainement pas**
	sairten-mahn pah
I don't think so	**Je ne crois pas**
	sher ner crwah pah
Not normally	**Normalement, non**
	normahl-mahn non
Sorry	**Je regrette**
	sher rer-gret

Reference

PUBLIC NOTICES

Priority road — End of priority road
right of way

RAPPEL

Reminder — maximum
Speed Limit

● Key words on signs for drivers, pedestrians, travellers, shoppers
and overnight guests.

ACCOTEMENTS NON STABILISÉS	Soft verges
ALLUMEZ VOS PHARES	Lights on
A LOUER	To let
APPUYER ICI	Press here
ARRIVÉES	Arrivals
ASCENSEUR	Lift
ATTENDEZ	Wait
ATTENTION	Caution
ATTENTION – CHIEN MÉCHANT	Beware of the dog
ATTENTION AUX TRAINS	Beware of the trains
AUTOROUTE	Motorway
A VENDRE	For sale
BAIGNADE INTERDITE	No swimming
BIÈRE PRESSION	Draught beer
BILLETS	Tickets
BROCANTE	Antique/second-hand/junk shop
CAISSE	Cash desk
CAMPING INTERDIT	No camping
CENTRE VILLE	Town centre
CHAMBRE À LOUER	Room to let
CHAMBRES LIBRES	Vacancies
CHAUD	Hot (tap)
CHAUSSÉE DÉFONCÉE	Bad surface (road)

CHAUSSÉE GLISSANTE	Slippery surface (road)
CHAUSSÉE RÉTRÉCIE	Road narrows
CHUTE DE PIERRES	Falling stones
CIRCUIT TOURISTIQUE	Scenic route
CLÉ MINUTE	Key cutting
COMPLET	Full – no vacancies
CONGÉ ANNUEL	Closed for holiday period
CONSIGNE	Left luggage
CYCLISTES	Bicycles
DAMES	Ladies
DÉFENSE D'AFFICHER	Bill posters will be prosecuted
DÉFENSE D'ENTRER SOUS PEINE D'AMENDE	Trespassers will be prosecuted
DÉPANNAGE	Emergency repairs
DÉPARTS	Departures
DÉVIATION	Diversion
DOUCHE	Shower
EAU NON POTABLE	Not for drinking (water)
EAU POTABLE	Drinking water
ÉCOLE	School
EMPRUNTEZ LE SOUTERRAIN	Take the subway
EN RÉCLAME	Special offer
ENTRÉE	Entrance
ENTRÉE GRATUITE	Free entry
ENTRÉE INTERDITE	No entry
ESCALIER	Stairs
ÉTAGE (PREMIER, DEUXIÈME)	Floor (first, second)
FEMMES	Ladies
FERMÉ (LE LUNDI)	Closed (on Mondays)
FERMETURE ANNUELLE	Closed for holidays
FEUX DE CIRCULATION	Traffic lights
FILE DE DROITE	Right hand lane
FILE DE GAUCHE	Left hand lane
FIN D'AUTOROUTE	End of motorway
FRAPPEZ	Knock
FROID	Cold (tap)
GARE ROUTIÈRE	Coach station
GARE SNCF	Railway station
GRATUIT	Free
HÔPITAL	Hospital
IL EST INTERDIT DE DOUBLER	No overtaking

IL EST INTERDIT DE FUMER	No smoking
IMPASSE	Cul-de-sac
INTERDIT	Forbidden
INTERDIT AUX PIÉTONS	No pedestrians
INTRODUISEZ VOTRE PIÈCE ICI	Insert coin here
JOUR DE FERMETURE	Closing day
LAVABOS	Washbasins/Toilets
LAVERIE AUTOMATIQUE	Launderette
LIBRE	Free
LOCATION (DE VOITURES)	(Car) Hire
LOCATIONS	Bookings
MESSIEURS	Gentlemen
MÉTRO	Underground train
NETTOYAGE À SEC, PRESSING	Dry cleaning
OBJETS TROUVÉS	Lost property
OCCASIONS	Bargains
OCCUPÉ	Occupied
OUVERT	Open
PARKING	Car park
PARLER ICI	Speak here
PASSAGE À NIVEAU	Level crossing
PASSAGE SOUTERRAIN	Subway
PAYEZ À LA SORTIE	Pay on your way out
PAYEZ ICI	Pay here
PÉAGE	Toll
PIÉTONS	Pedestrians
PLACES DEBOUT	Standing room
POIDS LOURDS	Heavy goods vehicles
PORTEUR	Porter
POUSSEZ	Push
PRIÈRE DE NE PAS (TOUCHER)	Please do not (touch)
PRIORITÉ À DROITE	Priority to the right
PRIVÉ	Private
PROPRIÉTÉ PRIVÉE	Private property
QUAI	Platform/Quay
RALENTIR	Slow down
RELÂCHE	Closed (for theatres, cinemas)
REMISES	Reductions
RENSEIGNEMENTS	Information

RÉSERVÉ AUX AUTOBUS	Buses only
RÉSERVÉ AUX CYCLISTES	Cycle lane
RESPECTEZ LES PELOUSES	Keep off the grass
REZ-DE-CHAUSSÉE	Ground floor
SABLES MOUVANTS	Quicksands
SALLE À MANGER	Dining room
SALLE D'ATTENTE	Waiting room
SENS UNIQUE	One way street
SERREZ À DROITE	Keep right
SOLDES	Sales
SONNEZ	Ring
SORTIE	Exit
SORTIE D'AUTOROUTE	Motorway exit
SORTIE DE CAMIONS	Lorry exit – Caution
SORTIE DE SECOURS	Emergency exit
SOUS-SOL	Basement
STATIONNEMENT INTERDIT	No waiting
STATIONNEMENT JOURS IMPAIRS	Parking allowed on odd days of the month (1st, 3rd, 5th . . .)
STATIONNEMENT JOURS PAIRS	Parking allowed on even days of the month (2nd, 4th, 6th . . .)
STATIONNEMENT LIMITÉ	Restricted waiting
SYNDICAT D'INITIATIVE	Tourist information office
TERRAIN MILITAIRE	Military zone
TIREZ	Pull
TOURNEZ LA POIGNÉE	Turn the handle
TOUTES DIRECTIONS	Through traffic
TRAVAUX	Works
TRAVERSEZ	Cross
TVA EN SUS	Plus VAT
VENTES	Sales
VIRAGES	Bends
VITESSE LIMITÉE	Speed limit
VOIE	Platform
VOIE SANS ISSUE	No through road
ZONE BLEUE	Parking discs required
ZONE PIÉTONNIÈRE	Pedestrian precinct

ABBREVIATIONS

A	autoroute	motorway
AJ	Auberge de jeunesse	Youth hostel
arr.	arrondissement	administrative district
CFF	Chemins de Fer Fédéraux	Swiss rail
ch.-l	chef-lieu	principal town in district
cl	centilitre	centilitre
D	(route) départementale	B-road
dep.	département	administrative county
douz.	douzaine	dozen
EGDF	Électricité et Gaz de France	French Electricity and Gas
E.U.	États-Unis	United States
F	fermé/franc/froid	off/franc/cold
faub.	faubourg	suburb
FB	Franc belge	Belgian franc
FF	Franc français	French franc
FFCC	Fédération Française de Camping et de Caravanning	French Federation of Camping and Caravanning
FS	Franc suisse	Swiss franc
HT	haute tension	high voltage
K/Kg(s)	kilogramme(s)	kilogram(s)
Km	kilomètre	kilometre
L	Livre sterling	pound sterling
l	litre	litre
M/MM	Monsieur/Messieurs	Mr/Messrs
Mlle/Mlles	Mademoiselle/Mesdemoiselles	Miss/the Misses
Mme/Mmes	Madame/Mesdames	Mrs/Mesdames
N	(route) nationale	A-road
O	Ouvert	On
PT	Postes et Télécommunications	the Post Office
RD	Route départementale	B-road
RER	Réseau express régional	fast coaches
RF	République française	French Republic
RN	Route nationale	A-road
SI	Syndicat d'initiative	Tourist information office
SNCB	Société Nationale des Chemins de Fer Belges	Belgian Rail

SNCF	Société Nationale des Chemins de Fer Français	French Rail
s.pref.	sous-préfecture	important town in a 'département'
SS	Sécurité Sociale	Social Security/ National Health
THT	**Très haute tension**	Very high voltage
TSVP	**Tournez s'il vous plaît**	Please turn over
t.t.c.	**toutes taxes comprises**	tax inclusive
TVA	**Taxe à la valeur ajoutée**	value added tax (VAT)

NUMBERS

Cardinal numbers

0	zéro	zehro
1	un	an
2	deux	der
3	trois	trwah
4	quatre	kat
5	cinq	sank
6	six	seess
7	sept	set
8	huit	weet
9	neuf	nerf
10	dix	deess
11	onze	onz
12	douze	dooz
13	treize	trez
14	quatorze	kattorz
15	quinze	kanz
16	seize	sez
17	dix-sept	dee-set
18	dix-huit	deezweet
19	dix-neuf	deez-nerf
20	vingt	van
21	vingt et un	vanteh an
22	vingt-deux	vant-der
23	vingt-trois	vant-trwah
24	vingt-quatre	vant-kat
25	vingt-cinq	vant-sank

26	vingt-six	vant-seess
27	vingt-sept	vant-set
28	vingt-huit	vant-weet
29	vingt-neuf	vant-nerf
30	trente	trahnt
31	trente et un	trahnteh an
35	trente-cinq	trahnt sank
38	trente-huit	trahnt weet
40	quarante	kah-rahnt
41	quarante et un	kahrahnteh an
45	quarante-cinq	kah-rahnt sank
48	quarante-huit	kah-rahnt weet
50	cinquante	sankahnt
55	cinquante-cinq	sankahnt sank
60	soixante	swah-sahnt
65	soixante-cinq	swah-sahnt sank
70	soixante-dix	swah-sahnt deess
75	soixante-quinze	swah-sahnt kanz
80	quatre-vingts	kat van
85	quatre-vingt-cinq	kat van sank
90	quatre-vingt-dix	kat van deess
95	quatre-vingt-quinze	kat van kanz
100	cent	sahn
101	cent un	sahn an
102	cent deux	sahn der
125	cent vingt-cinq	sahn vant sank
150	cent cinquante	sahn sankahnt
175	cent soixante-quinze	sahn swah-sahnt kanz
200	deux cents	der sahn
300	trois cents	trwah sahn
400	quatre cents	kat sahn
500	cinq cents	san sahn
1,000	mille	meel
1,500	mille cinq cents	meel san sahn
2,000	deux mille	der meel
5,000	cinq mille	san meel
10,000	dix mille	dee meel
100,000	cent mille	sahn meel
1,000,000	un million	an meel-yon

Ordinal numbers

1st	**premier (1e)**	prem-yeh
2nd	**deuxième (2e)**	derz-yem
3rd	**troisième (3e)**	trwahz-yem
4th	**quatrième (4e)**	katr-yem
5th	**cinquième (5e)**	sank-yem
6th	**sixième (6c)**	seess-yem
7th	**septième (7e)**	set-yem
8th	**huitième (8e)**	weet-yem
9th	**neuvième (9e)**	nerf-yem
10th	**dixième (10e)**	deess-yem
11th	**onzième (11e)**	onz-yem
12th	**douzième (12e)**	dooz-yem

TIME

What time is it?	**Quelle heure est-il?**
	keller eh-til
It's one o'clock	**Il est une heure**
	il eh ooner
It's ...	**Il est ...**
	il eh ...
two o'clock	**deux heures**
	der-zer
three o'clock	**trois heures**
	trwah-zer
four o'clock	**quatre heures**
	kat-er
in the morning	**du matin**
	doo mahtan
in the afternoon	**de l'après-midi**
	der lahpreh meedee
in the evening	**du soir**
	doo swah
It's ...	**Il est ...**
	il eh ...
noon	**midi**
	meedee
midnight	**minuit**
	meenwee

It's ...	Il est ...
	il eh ...
five past five	**cinq heures cinq**
	sanker sank
ten past five	**cinq heures dix**
	sanker deess
a quarter past five	**cinq heures et quart**
	sanker eh kar
twenty past five	**cinq heures vingt**
	sanker van
twenty-five past five	**cinq heures vingt-cinq**
	sanker vant sank
half past five	**cinq heures et demie**
	sanker eh der-me
twenty-five to six	**six heures moins vingt-cinq**
	seezer mwen vant sank
twenty to six	**six heures moins vingt**
	seezer mwen van
a quarter to six	**six heures moins le quart**
	seezer mwen ler kar
ten to six	**six heures moins dix**
	seezer mwen deess
five to six	**six heures moins cinq**
	seezer mwen sank
At what time ... (does the train leave)?	**A quelle heure ... (part le train)?**
	ah keller ... (par ler tran)
At ...	**A ...**
	ah ...
13.00	**treize heures**
	trez-er
14.05	**quatorze heures zéro cinq**
	kattorzer zehro sank
15.10	**quinze heures dix**
	kanzer deess
16.15	**seize heures quinze**
	sez-er kanz
17.20	**dix-sept heures vingt**
	dee-set er van
18.25	**dix-huit heures vingt-cinq**
	deezweet er vant sank
19.30	**dix-neuf heures trente**
	deez nerv-er trahnt

At...	A...
	ah ...
20.35	**vingt heures trente-cinq**
	vant-er trahnt sank
21.40	**vingt et une heures quarante**
	vant eh ooner kah-rahnt
22.45	**vingt-deux heures quarante-cinq**
	vant der zer kah-rahnt sank
23.50	**vingt-trois heures cinquante**
	vant trwah zer sankahnt
0.55	**zéro heure cinquante-cinq**
	zehro er sankahnt sank
in ten minutes	**dans dix minutes**
	dahn dee meenoot
in a quarter of an hour	**dans un quart d'heure**
	dahn-zan kar der
in half an hour	**dans une demi-heure**
	dahn-zoon der-me-er
in three quarters of an hour	**dans trois quarts d'heure**
	dahn trwah kar der

DAYS

Monday	**lundi**
	lerndee
Tuesday	**mardi**
	mardee
Wednesday	**mercredi**
	mairk-dee
Thursday	**jeudi**
	sher-dee
Friday	**vendredi**
	vahnd-dee
Saturday	**samedi**
	samdee
Sunday	**dimanche**
	deemahnsh
last Monday	**lundi dernier**
	lerndee dairn-yeh
next Tuesday	**mardi prochain**
	mardee proshan

on Wednesday	**mercredi**
	mairk-dee
on Thursdays	**le jeudi**
	ler sher-dee
until Friday	**jusqu'à vendredi**
	shooskah vahnd-dee
before Saturday	**avant samedi**
	ahvahn samdee
after Sunday	**après dimanche**
	ahpreh deemahnsh
the day before yesterday	**avant-hier**
	ahvahntee-air
two days ago	**il y a deux jours**
	il yah der shoor
yesterday	**hier**
	ee-air
yesterday morning	**hier matin**
	ee-air mahtan
yesterday afternoon	**hier après-midi**
	ee-air ahpreh-meedee
last night (evening)	**hier soir**
	ee-air swah
today	**aujourd' hui**
	o-shoordwee
this morning	**ce matin**
	ser mahtan
this afternoon	**cet après-midi**
	set ahpreh meedee
tonight	**ce soir**
	ser swah
tomorrow	**demain**
	der-man
tomorrow morning	**demain matin**
	der-man mahtan
tomorrow afternoon	**demain après-midi**
	der-man ahpreh meedee
tomorrow evening ⎤	**demain soir**
tomorrow night ⎦	der-man swah
the day after tomorrow	**après-demain**
	ahpreh der-man

MONTHS AND DATES

January	**janvier**
	shahnv-yeh
February	**février**
	fehvree-eh
March	**mars**
	marss
April	**avril**
	avreel
May	**mai**
	meh
June	**juin**
	shoo-an
July	**juillet**
	shwee-yeh
August	**août**
	oot
September	**septembre**
	septahmb
October	**octobre**
	octob
November	**novembre**
	novahmb
December	**décembre**
	dessahmb
in January	**au mois de janvier**
	o mwah der shahnv-yeh
until February	**jusqu'au mois de février**
	shoosko mwah der fehvree-eh
before March	**avant le mois de mars**
	ahvahn ler mwah der marss
after April	**après le mois d'avril**
	ahpreh ler mwah davreel
during May	**pendant le mois de mai**
	pahndahn ler mwah der meh
not until June	**pas avant le mois de juin**
	pah ahvahn ler mwah der shoo-an
the beginning of July	**le début juillet**
	ler dehboo shwee-yeh
the middle of August	**la mi-août**
	lah me-oot

the end of September	**la fin septembre** lah fan septahmb
last month	**le mois dernier** ler mwah dairn-yeh
this month	**ce mois-ci** ser mwah-see
next month	**le mois prochain** ler mwah proshan
in spring	**au printemps** o prantahn
in summer	**en été** ahn eh-teh
in autumn	**en automne** ahn oton
in winter	**en hiver** ahn eevair
this year	**cette année** set anneh
last year	**l'année dernière** lanneh dairn-yair
next year	**l'année prochaine** lanneh proshen
in 1982	**en mil neuf cent quatre-vingt-deux** ahn mil nerf sahn kat van der
in 1985	**en mil neuf cent quatre-vingt-cinq** ahn mil nerf sahn kat van sank
in 1990	**en mil neuf cent quatre-vingt-dix** ahn mil nerf sahn kat van deess
What's the date today?	**Quel jour sommes-nous?** kel shoor som noo
It's the 6th of March	**C'est le six mars** seh ler see marss
It's the 12th of April	**C'est le douze avril** seh ler dooz avreel
It's the 21st of August	**C'est le vingt et un août** seh le vanteh an oot

Public holidays in France and Belgium

● On these days, offices, shops and schools are closed.

1 January	**Jour de l'An**	New Year's Day
...	**Lundi de Pâques**	Easter Monday
1 May	**Fête du Travail**	Labour Day
...	**Ascension**	Ascension Day
...	**Lundi de Pentecôte**	Whit Monday
14 July	**Quatorze Juillet**	Bastille Day (France)
21 July	**Fête Nationale**	National Day (Belgium)
15 August	**Assomption**	Assumption Day
	Quinze Août	
1 November	**Toussaint**	All Saints Day
11 November	**Armistice**	Remembrance Day
25 December	**Noël**	Christmas Day
26 December	**Saint-Étienne**	St Stephen's Day (Belgium)

COUNTRIES AND NATIONALITIES

Countries

Australia	**(l') Australie**
	(l) ostrah-lee
Austria	**(l') Autriche**
	(l) otreesh
Belgium	**(la) Belgique**
	(lah) belsheek
Britain	**(la) Grande-Bretagne**
	(lah) grahnd brer-tan
Canada	**(le) Canada**
	(ler) canadah
East Africa	**(l') Afrique de l'Est**
	(l) ahfreek der lest
Eire	**(l') Irlande du Sud**
	(l) eerlahnd doo sood
England	**(l') Angleterre**
	(l) ahng-tair
France	**(la) France**
	(lah) frahns
Greece	**(la) Grèce**
	(lah) gress
India	**(l') Inde**
	(l) and

Italy	**(l') Italie**
	(l) eetah-lee
Luxembourg	**(le) Luxembourg**
	(ler) look-sahn-boor
Netherlands	**(la) Hollande**
	(lah) ollahnd
New Zealand	**(la) Nouvelle-Zélande**
	(lah) noovel zehlahnd
Northern Ireland	**(l') Irlande du Nord**
	(l) eerlahnd doo nor
Pakistan	**(le) Pakistan**
	(ler) pakistan
Portugal	**(le) Portugal**
	(ler) portoogal
Scotland	**(l') Écosse**
	(l) ehcoss
South Africa	**(l') Afrique du Sud**
	(l) ahfreek doo sood
Spain	**(l') Espagne**
	(l) espan
Switzerland	**(la) Suisse**
	(lah) sweess
United States	**(les) États-Unis**
	(leh-z) ehtah-zoonee
Wales	**(le) Pays de Galles**
	(ler) peh-ee der gal
West Germany	**(l') Allemagne de l'Ouest**
	(l) alman der loo-est
West Indies	**(les) Antilles**
	(leh-z) ahntee
in England	**en Angleterre**
	ahn ahng-tair
in Switzerland	**en Suisse**
	ahn sweess
in Pakistan	**au Pakistan**
	o pakistan
in Portugal	**au Portugal**
	o portoogal
in the United States	**aux États-Unis**
	o-zehtah-zoonee
in the West Indies	**aux Antilles**
	o-zahntee

Nationalities
[Use the first alternative for men, the second for women.]

American	**américain/américaine**
	american/ameriken
Australian	**australien/australienne**
	ostrahl-yan/ostrahl-yen
British	**britannique**
	britanneek
Canadian	**canadien/canadienne**
	canahdee-an/canahdee-en
East African	**est-africain/est-africaine**
	est-african/est-afriken
English	**anglais/anglaise**
	ahngleh/ahnglez
Indian	**indien/indienne**
	andee-an/andee-en
Irish	**irlandais/irlandaise**
	eerlahndeh/eerlahndez
a New Zealander	**néo-zélandais/néo-zélandaise**
	nay-o-zehlahn-deh/nay-o-zehlahndez
a Pakistani	**pakistanais/pakistanaise**
	pakistan-eh/pakistan-ez
Scots	**écossais/écossaise**
	eh-cosseh/eh-cossez
South African	**sud-africain/sud-africaine**
	sood-african/sood-afriken
Welsh	**gallois/galloise**
	gahlwah/gahlwaz
West Indian	**antillais/antillaise**
	ahntee-yeh/ahntee-yez

DEPARTMENT STORE GUIDE

Accessoires automobile	Car accessories
Accessoires cuisine	Kitchen gadgets
Accessoires mode	Fashion accessories
Alimentation	Food
Ameublement	Soft Furnishings
Articles de mode	Fashion articles
Articles de voyage	Travel articles
Arts ménagers	China, glassware, kitchenware
Bas	Stockings
Bijouterie	Jewellery
Blanc	Household linen
Bricolage	Do-it-yourself
Cadeaux	Gifts
Caisse	Cash desk
Camping	Camping
Ceintures	Belts
Chemiserie	Shirts
Chemises	Shirts
Chaussures	Shoes
Confection	Ready-to-wear
Coussins	Cushions
Couvertures	Blankets
Cravates	Ties
Crédits	Credit-Accounts
Dame(s)	Woman/women's wear
Deuxième	Second
Disques	Records
Éclairage	Lighting
Électro-ménager	Electrical appliances
Enfant(s)	Child/children
Entretien	Cleaning materials
Étage	Floor
Gaines	Girdles
Homme(s)	Man/men's wear
Jouets	Toys
Layette	Babywear
Librairie	Books
Linge maison	Household linen
Lingerie	Women's underwear
Literie	Bedding

Maquillage	Make-up
Maroquinerie	Leather goods
Mercerie	Haberdashery
Meubles	Furniture
Meubles de cuisine	Kitchen furniture
Mode(s)	Fashions
Pantoufles	Slippers
Papèterie	Stationery
Parfumerie	Perfumery
Photo(graphie)	Photography
Premier	First
Prêt-à-porter	Ready-to-wear
Produits de beauté	Beauty products
Pulls	Jumpers
Quatrième	Fourth
Quincaillerie	Hardware
Radio	Radio
Renseignements	Information
Revêtements de sol	Floor coverings
Rez-de-chaussée	Ground floor
Rideaux	Curtains
Service après-vente	Complaints, repairs
Sous-sol	Basement
Sous-vêtements	Underwear
Soutiens-gorge	Bras
Talon minute	Heel bar
Tapis	Carpets
Télévision	Television
Tissus	Fabrics
Tissus d'ameublement	Furnishing fabrics
Troisième	Third
Vaisselle	China
Verrerie	Glassware

CONVERSION TABLES

Read the centre column of these tables from right to left to convert from metric to imperial and from left to right to convert from imperial to metric e.g. 5 litres = 8.80 pints; 5 pints = 2.84 litres.

pints		litres		gallons		litres
1.76	1	0.57		0.22	1	4.55
3.52	2	1.14		0.44	2	9.09
5.28	3	1.70		0.66	3	13.64
7.07	4	2.27		0.88	4	18.18
8.80	5	2.84		1.00	5	22.73
10.56	6	3.41		1.32	6	27.28
12.32	7	3.98		1.54	7	31.82
14.08	8	4.55		1.76	8	36.37
15.84	9	5.11		1.98	9	40.91

ounces		grams		pounds		kilos
0.04	1	28.35		2.20	1	0.45
0.07	2	56.70		4.41	2	0.91
0.11	3	85.05		6.61	3	1.36
0.14	4	113.40		8.82	4	1.81
0.18	5	141.75		11.02	5	2.27
0.21	6	170.10		13.23	6	2.72
0.25	7	198.45		15.43	7	3.18
0.28	8	226.80		17.64	8	3.63
0.32	9	255.15		19.84	9	4.08

inches		centimetres		yards		metres
0.39	1	2.54		1.09	1	0.91
0.79	2	5.08		2.19	2	1.83
1.18	3	7.62		3.28	3	2.74
1.58	4	10.16		4.37	4	3.66
1.95	5	12.70		5.47	5	4.57
2.36	6	15.24		6.56	6	5.49
2.76	7	17.78		7.66	7	6.40
3.15	8	20.32		8.65	8	7.32
3.54	9	22.86		9.84	9	8.23

miles		kilometres
0.62	1	1.61
1.24	2	3.22
1.86	3	4.83
2.49	4	6.44
3.11	5	8.05
3.73	6	9.66
4.35	7	11.27
4.97	8	12.87
5.59	9	14.48

A quick way to convert kilometres to miles: divide by 8 and multiply by 5. To convert miles to kilometres: divide by 5 and multiply by 8.

fahrenheit (°F)	centigrade (°C)		lbs/ sq in	k/ sq cm
212°	100°	boiling point	18	1.3
100°	38°		20	1.4
98.4°	36.9°	body temperature	22	1.5
86°	30°		25	1.7
77°	25°		29	2.0
68°	20°		32	2.3
59°	15°		35	2.5
50°	10°		36	2.5
41°	5°		39	2.7
32°	0°	freezing point	40	2.8
14°	−10°		43	3.0
−4°	−20°		45	3.2
			46	3.2
			50	3.5
			60	4.2

To convert °C to °F: divide by 5, multiply by 9 and add 32. To convert °F to °C: subtract 32, divide by 9 and multiply by 5.

CLOTHING SIZES

Remember – always try on clothes before buying. Clothing sizes are usually unreliable.

women's dresses and suits
Europe	38	40	42	44	46	48
UK	32	34	36	38	40	42
USA	10	12	14	16	18	20

men's suits and coats
Europe	46	48	50	52	54	56
UK and USA	36	38	40	42	44	46

men's shirts
Europe	36	37	38	39	41	42	43
UK and USA	14	14½	15	15½	16	16½	17

socks
Europe	38–39	39–40	40–41	41–42	42–43
UK and USA	9½	10	10½	11	11½

shoes
Europe	34	35½	36½	38	39	41	42	43	44	45
UK	2	3	4	5	6	7	8	9	10	11
USA	3½	4½	5½	6½	7½	8½	9½	10½	11½	12½

Do it yourself

Some notes on the language

This section does not deal with 'grammar' as such. The purpose here is to explain some of the most obvious and elementary nuts and bolts of the language, based on the principal phrases included in the book. This information should enable you to produce numerous sentences of your own making.

There is no pronunciation guide in the first section, partly because it would get in the way of the explanations and partly because you have to do it yourself at this stage if you are serious – work out the pronunciation from all the earlier examples in the book.

THE

All nouns in French belong to one of two genders: masculine or feminine, irrespective of whether they refer to living beings or inanimate objects.

The	masculine	feminine	plural	
the address		l'adresse	les adresses	the addresses
the apple		la pomme	les pommes	the apples
the bill		l'addition	les additions	the bills
the cup of tea		la tasse de thé	les tasses de thé	the cups of tea
the glass of beer	le verre de bière		les verres de bière	the glasses of beer
the key		la clé	les clés	the keys
the luggage			les bagages	the luggage
the menu	le menu		les menus	the menus
the newspaper	le journal		les journaux	the newspapers
the receipt	le reçu		les reçus	the receipts
the sandwich	le sandwich		les sandwichs	the sandwiches
the suitcase		la valise	les valises	the suitcases
the telephone directory	l'annuaire téléphonique		les annuaires téléphoniques	the telephone directories
the timetable	l'horaire		les horaires	the timetables

Important things to remember

- *The* is **le** before a masculine noun, and **la** before a feminine noun.
- *The* is **l'** before masculine and feminine nouns which begin with a

vowel (*h* often counts as a vowel): **l'adresse (f)** and **l'horaire (m)**, when referring to a single thing.

- There is no way of predicting whether a noun is masculine or feminine. You have to learn and remember its gender. Obviously, if you are reading a word with **le** or **la** in front of it, you can detect its gender immediately: **le menu** is masculine (*m*. in dictionaries) and **la valise** is feminine (*f*. in dictionaries).

- Does it matter? Not unless you want to make a serious attempt to speak correctly and scratch beneath the surface of the language. You would be understood if you said **la menu**, or even **le horaire**, provided your pronunciation was good.

- *The* is always **les** before a noun in the plural.

- As a general rule, a noun adds an 's' to become plural, but this does not change its pronunciation: **clé** and **clés** sound the same. But watch out for many exceptions such as **journal/journaux**.

- In French, luggage is always regarded as plural. It is never used to mean a single item.

Practise saying and writing these sentences in French:

Have you got the key?	Avez-vous la clé?
Have you got the luggage?	Avez-vous . . . ?
Have you got the telephone directory?	
Have you got the menu?	
I'd like the key	Je voudrais la clé
I'd like the receipt	Je voudrais . . .
I'd like the bill	
I'd like the keys	
Where is the key?	Où est la clé?
Where is the timetable?	Où est . . . ?
Where is the address?	
Where is the suitcase?	
Where are the keys?	Où sont les clés?
Where are the sandwiches?	Où sont . . . ?
Where are the apples?	
Where are the suitcases?	
Where is the luggage?	Où sont . . . ?
Where can I get the key?	Où puis-je trouver la clé?
Where can I get the address?	Où puis-je trouver . . . ?
Where can I get the timetables?	

Now make up more sentences along the same lines.
Try adding *please*: **s'il vous plaît**, at the end.

A/AN

A/an	masculine	feminine	plural	some/any
an address		une adresse	des adresses	addresses
an apple		une pomme	des pommes	apples
a bill		une addition	des additions	bills
a cup of tea		une tasse de thé	des tasses de thé	cups of tea
a glass of beer	un verre de bière		des verres de bière	glasses of beer
a key		une clé	des clés	keys
...		...	des bagages	luggage
a menu	un menu		des menus	menus
a newspaper	un journal		des journaux	newspapers
a receipt	un reçu		des reçus	receipts
a sandwich	un sandwich		des sandwichs	sandwiches
a suitcase		une valise	des valise	suitcases
a telephone directory	un annuaire téléphonique		des annuaires téléphoniques	telephone directories
a timetable	un horaire		des horaires	timetables

Important things to remember

● *A* or *an* is always **un** before a masculine noun, and **une** before a feminine noun.

● *Some* or *any* is always **des** before a noun in the plural. In certain expressions in French, des is left out: see an example of this in the sentences marked with a * below.

Practise saying and writing these sentences in French:

Have you got a receipt?	Avez-vous ... ?
Have you got a menu?	
I'd like a telephone directory	Je voudrais ...
I'd like some sandwiches	
Where can I get some newspapers?	Où puis-je trouver ... ?
Where can I get a cup of tea?	
Is there a key?	Est-ce qu'il y a une clé?
Is there a timetable?	Est-ce qu'il y a ... ?
Is there a telephone directory?	
Is there a menu?	
Are there any keys?	Est-ce qu'il y a des clés?
Are there any newspapers?	Est-ce qu'il y a ... ?
Are there any sandwiches?	

Now make up more sentences along the same lines.

Then try these new phrases:
Je vais prendre ... (I'll have ...)
J'ai besoin de ... (I need ...)

I'll have a glass of beer	**Je vais prendre un verre de bière**
I'll have a cup of tea	**Je vais prendre ...**
I'll have some sandwiches	
I'll have some apples	
I need a cup of tea	**J'ai besoin d'une tasse de thé**
I need a key	**J'ai besoin d' ...**
*I need some newspapers	**J'ai besoin de journaux**
*I need some keys	**J'ai besoin de ...**
*I need some addresses	**J'ai besoin d' ...**
*I need some sandwiches	
*I need some suitcases	

SOME/ANY

In cases where some or any refer to more than one thing, such as
some/any ice-creams and *some/any tomatoes*, the word **des** is used as
explained earlier:

des glaces	some/any ice-creams
des tomates	some/any tomatoes

As a guide, you can usually *count* the number of containers or whole
items.
In cases where *some* refers to part of a whole thing or an indefinite
quantity, the word **des** cannot be used.
Look at the list below:

the bread	**le pain**	**du pain**	some bread
the ice-cream	**la glace**	**de la glace**	some ice-cream
the pineapple	**l'ananas (m)**	**de l'ananas**	some pineapple
the tomato	**la tomate**	**de la tomate**	some tomato
the water	**l'eau (f)**	**de l'eau**	some water
the wine	**le vin**	**du vin**	some wine

Important things to remember

● **Du** is used for masculine nouns.
● **De la** is used for feminine nouns.
● **De l'** is used for both masculine and feminine nouns which begin
with a vowel.

Can you complete the list below?

the aspirin	l'aspirine (f)	. . . some aspirin
the beer	la bière	. . . some beer
the cheese	le fromage	. . . some cheese
the coffee	le café	. . . some coffee
the lemonade	la limonade	. . . some lemonade
the tea	le thé	. . . some tea

Practise saying and writing these sentences in French:

Have you got some coffee?	Avez vous du café?
Have you got some ice-cream?	
Have you got some pineapple?	
I'd like some aspirin	Je voudrais de l'aspirine
I'd like some tomato	
I'd like some bread	
Is there any lemonade?	Est-ce qu'il y a de la limonade?
Is there any water?	
Is there any wine?	
Where can I get some cheese?	Où puis-je trouver du fromage?
Where can I get some ice-cream?	
Where can I get some water?	
I'll have some beer	Je vais prendre de la bière
I'll have some tea	
I'll have some coffee	

THIS AND THAT

One word in French: ça
If you don't know the French name for an object, just point and say:

Je voudrais ça	I'd like that
Je vais prendre ça	I'll have that
J'ai besoin de ça	I need this

HELPING OTHERS

You can help yourself with phrases such as:

I'd like . . . a sandwich	Je voudrais . . . un sandwich
Where can I get . . . a cup of tea?	Où puis-je trouver . . . une tasse de thé?
I'll have . . . a glass of beer	Je vais prendre . . . un verre de bière
I need . . : a receipt	J'ai besoin d' . . . une facture

If you come across a compatriot having trouble making himself understood, you should be able to speak to the French person on their behalf.

He'd like . . .	**Il voudrait un sandwich** il voodreh an sandwich
She'd like . . .	**Elle voudrait un sandwich** el voodreh an sandwich
Where can he get . . . ?	**Où peut-il trouver une tasse de thé?** oo per til trooveh oon tass der teh
Where can she get . . . ?	**Où peut-elle trouver une tasse de thé?** oo per tel trooveh oon tass der teh
He'll have . . .	**Il va prendre un verre de bière** il vah prahnd an vair der be-air
She'll have . . .	**Elle va prendre un verre de bière** el vah prahnd an vair der be-air
He needs . . .	**Il a besoin d'un reçu** il ah ber-zwan dan rer-soo
She needs . . .	**Elle a besoin d'un reçu** el ah ber-zwan dan rer-soo

You can also help a couple or a group if *they* are having difficulties. There are two French words for *they*: elles (women) and ils (men). When women and men are mixed, *they* are referred to as **ils.** If *they* are a married couple, for example, the word is **ils.**

They'd like . . .	**Ils voudraient du fromage** il voodreh doo fromash **Elles voudraient du fromage** el voodreh doo fromash
Where can they get . . . ?	**Où peuvent-ils trouver de l'aspirine?** oo perv til trooveh der laspeereen **Où peuvent-elles trouver de l'aspirine?** oo perv tel trooveh der laspeereen

They'll have . . .	**Ils vont prendre du vin**
	il von prahnd doo van
	Elles vont prendre du vin
	el von prahnd doo van
They need . . .	**Ils ont besoin d'eau**
	il zon ber-zwan do
	Elles ont besoin d'eau
	el zon ber-zwan do

What about the two of you? No problem. The word for *we* is **nous**.

We'd like . . .	**Nous voudrions du vin**
	noo voodree-on doo van
Where can we get . . . ?	**Où pouvons-nous trouver de l'eau?**
	oo poovon noo trooveh der lo
We'll have . . .	**Nous allons prendre de la bière**
	noo ahlon prahnd der lah be-air
We need . . .	**Nous avons besoin d'aspirine**
	noo zahvon ber-zwan daspeereen

Try writing out your own checklists for these four useful phrase-starters, like this:

Je voudrais . . .	**Nous voudrions . . .**
Il voudrait . . .	**Ils voudraient . . .**
Elle voudrait . . .	**Elles voudraient . . .**
Où puis-je trouver . . . ?	**Où . . . -nous trouver . . . ?**
Où peut-il trouver . . . ?	**Où . . . -ils trouver . . . ?**
Où peut-elle trouver . . . ?	**Où . . . -elles trouver . . . ?**

MORE PRACTICE

Here are some more French names of things. See how many different
sentences you can make up, using the various points of information
given earlier in this section.

		singular	plural
1	ashtray	cendrier (m)	cendriers
2	bag	sac (m)	sacs
3	broom	balai (m)	balais
4	car	voiture (f)	voitures
5	cigarette	cigarette (f)	cigarettes
6	corkscrew	tire-bouchon (m)	tire-bouchons
7	glove	gant (m)	gants
8	ice-cream	glace (f)	glaces
9	melon	melon (m)	melons
10	passport	passeport (m)	passeports
11	rag (dish cloth)	torchon (m)	torchons
12	salad	salade (f)	salades
13	saucepan	casserole (f)	casseroles
14	shoe	chaussure (f)	chaussures
15	stamp	timbre (m)	timbres
16	station	gare (f)	gares
17	street	rue (f)	rues
18	sunglasses		lunettes de soleil (f)
19	telephone	téléphone (m)	téléphones
20	ticket	billet (m)	billets

Index

Notes

avoir - have

partir - to leave

Notes

j'ai   nous avons
Tu as   vous avez
il a   ils ont

Être - to be
je suis   nous sommes
Tu es   vous êtes
il est   ils sont

Prendre - to take
je prends   nous prenons
Tu prends   vous prenez
il prend   ils prennent

Faire - to do, to make
je fais   nous faisons
Tu fais   vous faites
il fait   ils font

Aller - to go
je vais   nous allons
Tu vas   vous allez
il va   ils vont

C'est combien - how much

Ça fait combien "

Qu'est-ce c'est - what is it

Qu'est-ce que - what

Ou sont les toilettes

J'aimerais - I would like

Je prends un thé - I'll have

Je ne sais pas

Je ne comprends pas - understand

l'addition, s'il vous plaît

J'ai reservé une chambre

Pour aller à la gare ? How do I get
to the train station

Où se trouve

Il fant + infinitive

Quand ? When

Arthur Eperon
Travellers' France

Six major routes across France, taking in the best restaurants and hotels, visiting the most interesting out-of-the-way places. This detailed and up-to-the-minute handbook is for the traveller who wants more out of France than a mad dash down the motorway. Each of the six routes across the country is illustrated with a specially-commissioned two-colour map, and includes a host of information on where to eat and drink, where to take the children, where to stay, and how to get the most out of the towns and countryside.

Travellers' Italy

A whole variety of holiday routes to guarantee that you eat, drink, explore and relax in the places the Italians themselves would choose. The best places to sample local speciality foods and wines, spectacular scenery, facts the history books won't tell you, as well as the magnificent beaches and art treasures you'd expect. Arthur Eperon is one of the best-known travel writers in Europe and has an extensive knowledge of Italy and its food and wine. With an introduction by Frank Bough.

Companion Language Dictionaries

English – Français   French – Anglais
English – Deutsch   German – Englisch
English – Español   Spanish – Inglés
English – Italiano   Italian – Inglese

These pocket bilingual dictionaries have been especially designed for use by both English *and* French, German, Spanish and Italian speakers and are suitable for tourists, business travellers and students up to approximately O level. Each dictionary contains about 10,000 headwords; each entry contains a minimum of useful grammatical information such as gender of nouns, cases with German verbs etc. There is a pronunciation guide to both the foreign language and English headwords.

Harrap's New Pocket French and English Dictionary

The classic French/English and English/French reference for students and travellers, this edition contains some 4,500 entries in each language, including all the principal words in current use – recent additions to both languages, scientific terms, tourist expressions. Entries also contain phonetic renderings and examples of idiomatic usage.

A Multilingual Commercial Dictionary

Some 3,000 words and phrases in common commercial use are listed in English, French, German, Spanish and Portugese followed by their translation in the other languages. The equivalent American expression is also included where relevant. Simple to use and invaluable for everyday reference, the dictionary covers terms used throughout banking, accounting, insurance, shipping, export and import and international trade.

Now available to accompany this phrase book
A specially recorded, 60-minute

Audio cassette

Why a cassette?

This cassette has been produced to enable phrase book users to
become familiar with

- the pronunciation and intonation of French, preferably before
  leaving for France
- the pronunciation guide provided in the book
- the likely reactions to their questions in French

What is on the cassette?

Selected parts of nearly all sections of the phrase book have
been recorded by a native speaker. There is no separate script:
the recording tells you which page in the phrase book to turn to.
It is ideal for using in the car or for listening to while doing jobs
around the house.

ALL LIKELY REACTIONS, and the key phrases to understand
are recorded without pauses for you to repeat, so that you can
just get used to listening to them.

All other phrases (WHAT TO SAY) can be repeated out loud,
and pauses have been left on the cassette so that you can
imitate the speaker without having to stop the tape.

This cassette has been recorded and produced by PRINTAWAY
LIMITED for PAN BOOKS LIMITED and is *only* available from

Printaway Publishing,

Seton Works,

Cockenzie, East Lothian

Tel: Port Seton (0875) 811401

Price £3.00 (incl VAT, P&P)
Also available in German, Spanish and Italian.